The Ultimate Egg Cooker Recipe Book

Delicious Foolproof Recipes Using Your Electric Egg Cooker

Marilyn Haugen

and

Jennifer Williams

ISBN: 978-0-9982470-0-7

Published by Seven Island Press
Madison, WI
(608) 285-2021
www.sevenislandpress.com

Manufactured in the United States of America

Table of Contents

Acknowledgments

For my mother, who instilled in me the love of cooking. Her endless support and encouragement taught me that you can accomplish anything.

- Marilyn Haugen

Introduction

Not only do we love the taste of eggs in a variety of dishes, but eggs are good for us too. They are a great source of protein, which is an important part of our diet. Along with the protein they also contain amino acids which are very important for vegetarian diets.

Eggs also contain fats, the majority of which are unsaturated heart-healthy fats. They also contain vitamins, such as B12 and D, and minerals, such as iodine, all of which are essential in our diets.

All this before we even start with the delicious, mouthwatering recipes for appetizers, breakfast, main dishes, salads, side dishes and special diets.

If you are one of those people who know that a good breakfast or a healthy snack is the way to start your day but struggle for time and ideas on what to make, we know you will enjoy this fun and fast way to make a delicious breakfast dishes. A great breakfast gives your body essential fuel and nutrients to power you through the day. Breakfast gives you an energy boost, powers the brain and helps you to lose weight or keep it off.

But don't stop at just breakfast. Make eggs your new favorite food for a protein-packed, quick, easy and portable lunch or midday snack. If you do one good thing for yourself and your family, make a batch of hard-boiled eggs. Cool and peel them. Then wrap your eggs in an airtight container and refrigerate them for quick and easy meals during the week.

There are so many ways to cook eggs including boiling, poaching and scrambling. And an even larger number of ways that you can incorporate them into your meals.

If you also want to get more vegetables into your diet, the electric eggs cookers can help with that too. These little gems are just perfect for steaming vegetables to incorporate into your favorite eggs dishes. You can even use the cooker to make a single serving of steamed vegetables to go with any meal.

Not only do you have the simplicity of making these delicious foolproof recipes all in one cooker, but you can do it without adding additional oils and unhealthy fats to cook them. Steaming also helps retain many of their nutrients.

You have so many options available for quick, easy and nutritious meals and this book is designed to give you many great recipes.

EGG COOKER BASICS

The recipes in this book were developed using an egg cooker that cooks 6 boiled eggs, 2 poached eggs and 2 egg omelets and scrambled eggs. The recipes can readily be increased or decreased depending upon the size of your egg cooker or your personal preferences.

HARD-BOILED EGGS

If you've ever tried to make soft, medium or hard-boiled eggs you know that, while it may sound simple, it can be tricky to get a perfectly boiled egg. Additionally, getting perfectly peeled eggs becomes an even bigger challenge. The egg cookers make all of these steps, easy, quick and foolproof.

POACHED EGGS

Do you love eggs benedict but find poaching eggs to be time consuming, with less than perfect results? The eggs cookers make poaching eggs so simple that you can make your eggs benedict or add this healthy way of cooking eggs to other dishes.

OMELETS AND SCRAMBLED EGGS

You can even make omelets or scrambled eggs in the egg cooker without frying in extra oils or butter. This recipe book contains instructions on making the perfect omelet or scrambled eggs including adding additional ingredients such as cheese, vegetables and meats to your dishes.

STEAMED VEGETABLES

Making a quick and delicious meal just keeps getting better with your egg cooker where you can steam fresh vegetables to add to omelets, scrambled eggs, salads and even as a quick side dish.

Make Meals Even Easier

College students, busy moms, teenagers and so many people on the go find it either too time consuming or cumbersome to make a good meal for themselves.

*   Several of these recipes can be made ahead of time, refrigerated or frozen, and then finished just before serving, making meal preparation even easier.

*   With these delicious recipes and an egg cooker, your morning meal is easy and satisfying and it's ready in under 10 minutes and clean-up is a breeze.

*   You may even move some of the preparation work ahead of time making a great breakfast, ready to go lunch or an easy weeknight meal delicious and nutritious.

*   If you ever wondered what to bring to a potluck, you will find quick solutions in this recipe book and your egg cooker.

GETTING STARTED

Electric Egg Cookers: The recipes in this book have been designed to work with an electric egg cooker. You will find some of the directions very similar between recipes. That is because it really just takes a few simple steps to get your eggs ready to go. Also, I personally do not like reading a recipe that continually refers me back to the appliance manufacturer's instructions of some other random place in the book– I want it all in one spot – hopefully you will too.

Other Cooking Methods: These recipes can also be prepared with non-electric egg cookers or your good old fashioned pots and pans. You will just need to alter the directions accordingly and it may take longer to prepare.

Utensils and tools: We recommend using nylon or any other non-metal utensil when using your egg cooker to avoid scratching and damaging the surface. You will want to have a hot pad handy for transferring your eggs to a serving plate.

Ingredients: You will need to have a non-stick cooking spray on hand for the egg cooking trays. Spray the trays and then wipe up any excess with a paper towel.

Fresh herbs are also a wonderful to have on hand for any recipe. If you do need to substitute dried for fresh, reduce the amount of dried by one-third.

In our recipes we occasionally use a specific brand or type of ingredient in the recipe. You can, of course, substitute these with your favorite ingredients, local brand or whatever you have on hand in the kitchen.

Now Let's Get Cooking!

Appetizers

CLASSIC DEVILED EGGS

SMOKED SALMON DEVILED EGGS

MEDITERRANEAN-INSPIRED DEVILED EGGS

GUACAMOLE DEVILED EGGS

PARMESAN AND ARTICHOKE DEVILED EGGS

MINI AVOCADO AND EGG PARFAITS

PROSCIUTTO AND EGG CROSTINI

MINI EGG SALAD SANDWICHES

SMOKED SALMON AND EGG CANAPES

CRAB AND CREAM CHEESE STUFFED PASTRY PUFFS

CRAB SALAD STUFFED EGGS

SPICY CHEESE AND SPINACH STUFFED EGGS

PICKLED EGGS AND PROSCIUTTO CROSTINI

PENNSYLVANIA DUTCH PICKLED BEETS AND EGGS

Classic Deviled Eggs

Deviled eggs are the perfect appetizer for any party. Allow for 2 deviled egg halves per person and adjust the amount depending upon how many other appetizers you are serving. Just make sure you make enough because they will disappear quickly!

Makes 12 Appetizers

6	eggs
1/4 cup	real mayonnaise
1 tsp	white vinegar
1 tsp	prepared mustard
	Kosher salt and freshly ground black pepper
	Hungarian paprika

1. Pierce the bottom of each egg. Fill water in the measuring container to the "Hard" line and pour into the cooker. Place the eggs in the boiling tray bottom-side up. Cover and press the Power button. When the cooker beeps, transfer eggs to a bowl of cold water until cool enough to handle. Peel eggs under cold running water; dry with a paper towel. Slice eggs in half lengthwise. Transfer yolks to a medium bowl. Arrange egg whites on a serving platter, cut side up.
2. Using a fork, mash the egg yolks into a fine crumble. Add mayonnaise, vinegar and mustard, mixing well. Season to taste with salt and pepper. Using a spoon, transfer heaping spoonfuls of the egg mixture into the egg whites. Sprinkle with paprika. Serve immediately. Deviled eggs can be refrigerated up to 1 day; let stand at room temperature before serving.

Tip
* Deviled eggs can be refrigerated up to 1 day; let stand at room temperature for 30 minutes before serving.

(Continued on next page)

Deviled Egg Variations (continued)

You have now perfected the classic deviled egg. It's time to spread those wings and add some unique variations to your deviled eggs. With this base recipe you can mix and match these toppings depending upon the occasion and your personal tastes.

---

* ***Bacon and Chive Deviled Eggs:*** Substitute 1/4 cup sour cream and for the 3 tbsp of the real mayonnaise. Eliminate the vinegar and mustard. Add 6 strips cooked and crumbled bacon and 1/4 cup chopped chives. Add 5 strips of bacon and 3 tbsp chives to the egg mixture and follow the original method. Garnish tops of eggs with remaining bacon and chives.
* ***Southwestern Deviled Eggs:*** Substitute dried taco seasoning in place of the mustard. Add 1 tbsp diced sun-dried tomatoes. Garnish with diced green onions.

* Substitute the prepared mustard with Dijon, grainy or pub-style mustard.
* Use pickle juice instead of the white vinegar for a tangy flavor twist.
* Add 1/2 tsp Sriracha, or more to taste, instead of the prepared mustard.
* Add 1 tbsp diced green olives. Garnish with diced pimientos.
* Add 1 jalapeño, seeded and diced and 1 tsp cumin. Garnish with fresh cilantro.
* Add 2 tbsp crumbled bleu cheese to the egg yolk mixture and reduce the mayonnaise to 2 tbsp. Garnish with fresh oregano leaves.
* Add 1-1/2 tbsp diced ham and add 1 tbsp finely shredded cheddar cheese.

Smoked Salmon Deviled Eggs

Delicate smoked salmon, cream cheese and chives make these eggs fit for a perfect brunch party. Garnished with capers and they truly make a delicate dish.

Makes 16 Appetizers

6	eggs
1/2 cup	sour cream
3 tbsp	cream cheese, room temperature
2 tbsp	real mayonnaise
1 tbsp	lemon juice
3 tbsp	minced chives, divided
4 oz	smoked salmon, minced
1 tsp	kosher salt
1/2 tsp	freshly ground black pepper
2 tbsp	small capers

1. Pierce the bottom of each egg. Fill water in the measuring container to the "Hard" line and pour into the cooker. Place the eggs in the boiling tray bottom-side up. Cover and press the Power button. When the cooker beeps, transfer eggs to a bowl of cold water until cool enough to handle. Peel eggs under cold running water; dry with a paper towel. Slice eggs in half lengthwise. Transfer yolks to a medium bowl. Arrange egg whites on a serving platter, cut side up.

2. In the medium bowl with the egg yolks, add the sour cream, cream cheese, mayonnaise, lemon juice, 2 tbsp chives, smoked salmon, salt and pepper. Using an immersion blender or hand mixer, beat the mixture until combined and smooth. Using a spoon, transfer heaping spoonfuls of the egg mixture into the egg whites. Garnish with remaining chives and capers. Serve immediately.

Tips
* Cover deviled eggs with plastic wrap and refrigerate 30 minutes before serving to meld flavors.
* Deviled eggs can be refrigerated up to 1 day; let stand at room temperature before serving.

Mediterranean-Inspired Deviled Eggs

Slow down and enjoy the sun-dried tomatoes and feta cheese in these appetizing deviled eggs and then picture yourself on a sun-drenched beach in the Mediterranean.

Makes 12 Appetizers

6	eggs
1/4 cup	crumbled feta cheese
1/4 cup	diced sun-dried tomatoes
3 tbsp	Greek yogurt
1 tbsp	heavy cream
1/8 tsp	celery salt
1 tbsp	white vinegar
	Kosher salt and freshly ground black pepper
	Fresh mint leaves

1. Pierce the bottom of each egg. Fill water in the measuring container to the "Hard" line and pour into the cooker. Place the eggs in the boiling tray bottom-side up. Cover and press the Power button. When the cooker beeps, transfer eggs to a bowl of cold water until cool enough to handle. Peel eggs under cold running water; dry with a paper towel. Slice eggs in half lengthwise. Transfer yolks to a medium bowl. Arrange egg whites on a serving platter, cut side up.
2. Using a fork, mash the egg yolks into a fine crumble. Add the feta cheese, sun-dried tomatoes, yogurt, cream, celery salt and vinegar, mixing well. Season to taste with salt and pepper. Using a spoon, transfer heaping spoonfuls of the mixture into the egg whites. Garnish with mint leaves. Serve immediately or refrigerate until ready to serve.

Tip
* The egg mixture will still be chunky after mixing. It is not necessary to mix the filling until smooth.

Variations
* Substitute crumbled bleu cheese for the feta cheese.
* Add 1 tbsp diced Kalamata olives to the mixture or use as a garnish in place of the mint leaves.

Guacamole Deviled Eggs

Get ready for some amazing green eggs and ham, oh Sam I am. Loaded with avocado, eggs and garnished with bacon, these deviled eggs are a real treat.

Makes 24 Appetizers

12	eggs
1/3 cup	mayonnaise
1	medium avocado, peeled and pitted, about 1/3 cup mashed
2 tbsp	lemon juice
1-1/2 tbsp	Dijon mustard
	Kosher salt and freshly ground black pepper
4	slices crisp cooked bacon, crumbled

1. Pierce the bottom of each egg. Fill water in the measuring container to the "Hard" line and pour into the cooker. Place the eggs in the boiling tray bottom-side up. Cover and press the Power button. When the cooker beeps, transfer eggs to a bowl of cold water until cool enough to handle. Peel eggs under cold running water; dry with a paper towel. Slice eggs in half lengthwise. Transfer yolks to a medium bowl. Arrange egg whites on a serving platter, cut side up.
2. Using a fork, mash the egg yolks into a fine crumble. Add mayonnaise, avocado, lemon juice and mustard mixing well. Season to taste with salt and pepper. Using a spoon, transfer heaping spoonfuls of the egg mixture into the egg whites. Garnish with crumbled bacon. Serve immediately.

Tips
* Deviled eggs can be refrigerated up to 1 day; let stand at room temperature before serving.
* 1/2 of a lemon will yield about 2 tbsp fresh lemon juice.

Parmesan and Artichoke Deviled Eggs

If you are a fan of artichoke dip, then look no further for this mouthwatering twist on your favorite dip.

Makes 12 Appetizers

6	hard-boiled eggs, cooled
1/4 cup	grated Parmesan cheese
2 tbsp	diced marinated artichoke hearts (from a jar)
1 tbsp	capers
2 tbsp	real mayonnaise
2 tbsp	heavy cream
1 tbsp	white vinegar
	Kosher salt and freshly ground black pepper
	Fresh thyme leaves

1. Pierce the bottom of each egg. Fill water in the measuring container to the "Hard" line and pour into the cooker. Place the eggs in the boiling tray bottom-side up. Cover and press the Power button. When the cooker beeps, transfer eggs to a bowl of cold water until cool enough to handle. Peel eggs under cold running water; dry with a paper towel. Slice eggs in half lengthwise. Transfer yolks to a medium bowl. Arrange egg whites on a serving platter, cut side up.
2. Using a fork, mash the egg yolks into a fine crumble. Add the parmesan cheese, artichokes, capers, mayonnaise, cream and vinegar, mixing well. Season to taste with salt and pepper. Using a spoon, transfer heaping spoonfuls of the mixture into the egg whites. Garnish with thyme leaves. Serve immediately or refrigerate until ready to serve.

Tips
* Marinated artichokes can be found in jars ranging from 6 oz to 12 oz. You can serve the remaining artichokes on an antipasto platter for your guests.
* You can select only the amount of artichokes you need for this recipe in the salad bar counter of your grocery store.

Mini Avocado and Egg Parfaits

Get ready to impress your guests with these delectable, show-stopping appetizers.

Makes 6 Appetizers

6 - 2.5 oz mini parfait glasses
Mini dessert spoons
Piping bag

2	eggs
1	medium avocado, diced
2 tbsp	minced red onion
2-1/2 tsp	lemon juice
3/4 tsp	chopped fresh dill
	Kosher salt and freshly cracked black pepper
1/2 cup	sour cream
1	roma tomato, seeded and finely chopped
	Crackers

1. Pierce the bottom of each egg. Fill water in the measuring container to the "Hard" line and pour into the cooker. Place the eggs in the boiling tray bottom-side up. Cover and press the Power button. When the cooker beeps, transfer eggs to a bowl of cold water until cool enough to handle. Peel eggs under cold running water; dry with a paper towel. Finely chop egg and set aside.
2. In a small bowl, add avocado, red onion, lemon juice and dill. Using a fork, mash the mixture until coarsely combined. Season to taste with salt and pepper.
3. Spoon sour cream into piping bag. Pipe sour cream into parfait glasses, dividing amounts evenly.
4. Transfer spoonfuls of avocado mixture over sour cream. Sprinkle tomatoes and eggs over avocado mixture. Serve with mini dessert spoons and crackers.

Variation
* Garnish with 3 tsp of black or salmon caviar on top of the eggs.

Prosciutto and Egg Crostini

Layers of prosciutto, sliced hard-boiled eggs and a spicy mayonnaise grace pumpernickel toasts in this fun and delicious appetizer.

Makes 8 Appetizers

4	eggs
1/3 cup	mayonnaise
1 tbsp	Sriracha or other hot pepper sauce
	Kosher salt and freshly ground black pepper
8	slices cocktail pumpernickel bread, toasted
3	leaves Bibb lettuce, torn into 8 pieces
8	slices prosciutto

1. Pierce the bottom of each egg. Fill water in the measuring container to the "Hard" line and pour into the cooker. Place the eggs in the boiling tray bottom-side up. Cover and press the Power button. When the cooker beeps, transfer eggs to a bowl of cold water until cool enough to handle. Peel eggs under cold running water; dry with a paper towel. Thinly slice the eggs crosswise; reserve or discard end pieces.
2. In a small bowl, add mayonnaise and Sriracha, mixing well. Season to taste with salt and pepper.
3. Spread the mayonnaise mixture on each slice of bread. Top with a piece of lettuce. Arrange 2 slices of egg, overlapping slightly, and a piece of prosciutto, folded or twisted to fit on the top. Serve.

Tips
* You can use a slice of regular pumpernickel bread in place of the cocktail size. Cut bread into 1/3- to 1/2-inch thick slices, trim crusts and cut into 2-inch squares.
* Rye bread is also a nice substitute for the pumpernickel. Follow the tip above for cutting the pumpernickel to size.

Mini Egg Salad Sandwiches

So simple, yet so tasty. These delicate little sandwiches are filled with an egg salad blend that gets a little bit of acid from the lemon juice that makes all of the flavors pop.

Makes 12 Appetizers

6	eggs
1/4 cup	real mayonnaise
1 tbsp	chopped fresh chives
1 tbsp	prepared mustard
1 1/2 tsp	fresh lemon juice
	Kosher salt and freshly ground black pepper
6	slices sourdough bread, crusts trimmed
	Festive tooth pics (optional)

1. Pierce the bottom of each egg. Fill water in the measuring container to the "Hard" line and pour into the cooker. Place the eggs in the boiling tray bottom-side up. Cover and press the Power button. When the cooker beeps, transfer eggs to a bowl of cold water until cool enough to handle. Peel eggs under cold running water. Return eggs to cold water and let stand until cold, changing water as needed.
2. Finely chop the eggs and add to a medium bowl. Add the mayonnaise, chives, mustard and lemon juice, mixing well. Season to taste with salt and pepper, mixing to blend. Spread the egg salad on 3 slices. Add the remaining bread to the top of each spread side to make a sandwich. Cut each sandwich into 4 wedges. Add festive tooth pics, if using, to the secure each wedge and transfer to a serving platter.

Tips
* You can estimate 2 mini sandwiches per guest when these are served with an assortment of appetizers.
* This recipe is easily doubled. You will just need to make the eggs in two batches, or if you have a larger cooker that accommodates 12 eggs you are all set to go.

Smoked Salmon and Egg Canapes

Buttery smoked salmon rosettes grace a savory spread on cocktail bread slices for these impressive and stylish appetizers.

Makes 12 Appetizers

1	egg
1/2 cup	real mayonnaise
2	small sweet pickles (gherkins), minced
1 tbsp	finely chopped green chives
12	slices cocktail pumpernickel bread, toasted
12	small pieces, thinly sliced smoked salmon
1 tbsp	dill sprigs
	Black caviar (optional)

1. Pierce the bottom of the egg. Fill water in the measuring container to the "Hard" line and pour into the cooker. Place the egg in the boiling tray bottom-side up. Cover and press the Power button. When the cooker beeps, transfer egg to a bowl of cold water until cool enough to handle. Peel egg under cold running water; dry with a paper towel. Finely chop egg.
2. In a small bowl, add the eggs, mayonnaise, pickles and chives, mixing well.
3. Spread mixture on pumpernickel slices. Roll up salmon slices and curl out top edges to form a rose shape. Arrange salmon rosettes on top of spread. Garnish with dill sprigs and caviar (if using).

Make Ahead

* *3 Days Ahead of Time:* The egg spread can be prepared and refrigerated in an airtight container up to 3 days ahead of time. Let stand at room temperature for 30 minutes before spreading on toasts to make spreading easier.

* *1 Day Ahead of Time:* The pumpernickel bread can be toasted and refrigerated in an airtight container up to 1 day ahead of time.

Crab and Cream Cheese Stuffed Pastry Puffs

Start with delicate miniature pastry puffs and then stuff them with lump crabmeat, eggs and seasonings and you have an appetizer that will become an all-time favorite.

Make 48 Appetizers

Puffs

1 cup	water
1/2 cup	butter
1 cup	all-purpose flour
4	eggs

Filling

4	hard-boiled eggs, finely chopped (see Step 1, page 14)
1	6-oz can lump crabmeat, drained
1	4-oz block cream cheese, softened
1/4 cup	mayonnaise
2 tbsp	finely chopped red onion
2 tbsp	prepared horseradish, drained
	Minced fresh parsley

1. *Puffs:* Preheat oven to 400°F. In a large saucepan, heat water and butter to boiling. Add flour, stirring, and reduce heat to low. Continue stirring about 1 minute or until mixture forms a ball. Remove from the heat and add eggs, beating until smooth. Drop dough by 1 tablespoonful onto baking sheet. Bake 20 to 25 minutes, or until puffed and golden brown. Transfer pan to a wire rack and let stand about 30 minutes, or until cool.
2. *Filling:* Meanwhile, in a large bowl, add eggs, crabmeat, cream cheese, mayonnaise, onion and horseradish.
3. Cut off top half of each pastry puff; set top aside. Spoon a heaping spoonful of crabmeat filling onto the bottom half of each puff. Garnish with parsley and replace tops. Serve immediately.

Make Ahead
* *3 Days Ahead of Time:* The puffs can be made ahead of time, covered and stored at room temperature for up to 3 days. Fill puffs just before serving.
* *1 Day Ahead of Time:* The filling can be made 1 day ahead of time. Cover and refrigerate. Assemble puffs just be serving.

Crab Salad Stuffed Eggs

Sweet and succulent lump crab meat is combined with hard boiled eggs, crunchy celery and folded into a mustard yogurt dressing.

Makes 16 Appetizers

8	eggs
1 tsp	lime juice
2 tbsp	extra virgin olive oil
3 tbsp	plain Greek yogurt
1	6-oz can lump crabmeat, drained
1/4 cup	finely chopped celery (about 3 stalks)
1 tsp	ground mustard
	Kosher salt and freshly ground black pepper
	12 fresh asparagus tips (optional)

1. Pierce the bottom of each egg. Fill water in the measuring container to the "Hard" line and pour into the cooker. Place the eggs in the boiling tray bottom-side up. Cover and press the Power button. When the cooker beeps, transfer eggs to a bowl of cold water until cool enough to handle. Peel eggs under cold running water; dry with a paper towel. Slice eggs in half lengthwise. Transfer yolks to a medium bowl. Arrange egg whites on a serving platter, cut side up.

2. Using a fork, mash the egg yolks into a fine crumble. Set aside 1 tbsp crumbled yolks. To the remaining yolks, add lime juice and olive oil, whisking well. Add yogurt, crabmeat, celery and mustard, stirring gently until combined. Season to taste with salt and pepper. Using a spoon, transfer heaping spoonfuls of the egg and crab mixture into the egg whites. Garnish with reserved egg yolks. Insert an asparagus tip at an angle, cut side down, into the filling, if using. Serve immediately.

Variation

* Substitute 1 medium shallot, finely chopped (about 3 tbsp) in place of the celery and 4 to 5 strands saffron in place of the mustard.

Spicy Cheese and Spinach Stuffed Eggs

A creamy duo of cheese teams up with chopped spinach a bit of spice for an interesting twist in these devilish eggs.

Make 24 Appetizers

12	eggs
3/4 cup	frozen chopped spinach, thawed and drained
1	4 oz block cream cheese, softened
1/3 cup	grated parmesan cheese
2 tbsp	chopped green onions
1/2 tsp	seasoned salt, such as Old Bay Seasoning
1/8 tsp	cayenne pepper
	Fresh flat-leaf parsley

1. Pierce the bottom of each egg. Fill water in the measuring container to the "Hard" line and pour into the cooker. Place the eggs in the boiling tray bottom-side up. Cover and press the Power button. When the cooker beeps, transfer eggs to a bowl of cold water until cool enough to handle. Peel eggs under cold running water; dry with a paper towel. Slice eggs in half lengthwise. Transfer yolks to a medium bowl. Arrange egg whites on a serving platter, cut side up.

2. Using a fork, mash the egg yolks into a fine crumble. Add the spinach, cream cheese, parmesan, green onions, salt and pepper to the egg yolks, mixing well. Using a spoon, transfer heaping spoonfuls of the spinach mixture into the egg whites. Garnish with parsley. Refrigerate for 30 minutes before serving.

Tip

* Use a pastry bag fitted with a large star shaped tip and fill the bag with the spinach and egg mixture. Pipe the mixture into the egg whites for a more festive finish.

Pickled Eggs and Sausage on Crostini

Pickled egg spread adds a tangy twist to toasted garlic bread and savory prosciutto.

Makes 12 Appetizers

1/2 cup	apple cider vinegar
1/2 cup	white vinegar
2 tsp	pickling spices
1 tsp	granulated sugar
1-1/2 tsp	kosher salt
6	eggs
12	1 inch slices of Linguiça sausage
1/3 cup	real mayonnaise
1/4 cup	finely chopped fresh chives
3 tbsp	finely chopped fresh parsley, divided
12	slices French bread, about 1/2-inch thick
3 tbsp	virgin olive oil
2	cloves garlic

1. In a medium saucepan, add vinegars, spices, sugar, salt and 1/2 cup water; heat to simmering. Remove from heat and let stand until cool.
2. Pierce the bottom of each egg. Fill water in the measuring container to the "Hard" line and pour into the cooker. Place the eggs in the boiling tray bottom-side up. Cover and press the Power button. When the cooker beeps, transfer eggs to a bowl of cold water until cool enough to handle. Discard water, peel eggs under cold running water and return to the bowl. Add sausage pieces. Pour in vinegar mixture. Cover and refrigerate for 12 to 15 hours. The eggs can be pickled and refrigerated up to 1 week ahead of time.
3. Remove eggs from pickling liquid and reserve liquid. Dry eggs with a paper towel. Coarsely chop eggs and transfer them to a medium bowl. Add mayonnaise, chives and 2 tbsp parsley, mixing well. Add reserved pickling liquid, 1 tsp at a time to taste, if desired.
4. Preheat oven to 425°F. Transfer bread slices to a baking sheet. Brush slices with oil. Toast bread 5 minutes, or until golden brown. Rub top with garlic cloves. Let cool. Spread egg mixture on top of bread slices. Top with sausage and garnish with parsley.

Pennsylvania Dutch Pickled Beets and Eggs

There is a reason why some recipes stand the test of time and these colorful and incredibly tasty pickled eggs with beets and onions is a prime example. You owe it to yourself and your guests to give these delicacies a try.

Makes 12 Appetizers

6	eggs
1	16-oz can sliced beets with liquids
1/2 cup	granulated sugar
1/2 cup	apple cider vinegar
6	whole black peppercorns
6	whole allspice berries
1	small onion, sliced

1. Pierce the bottom of each egg. Fill water in the measuring container to the "Hard" line and pour into the cooker. Place the eggs in the boiling tray bottom-side up. Cover and press the Power button. When the cooker beeps, transfer eggs to a bowl of cold water until cool. Discard water, peel eggs under cold running water and return to the bowl.
2. Meanwhile, in a large saucepan, add beet liquid, sugar, vinegar, peppercorns and allspice and cook, stirring, over medium-high heat until boiling and sugar has dissolved. Remove from heat. Add eggs and onion to the saucepan, turning to coat eggs and onions completely. Add beets, stirring. Cover and refrigerate for 1 to 3 days, turning occasionally, or until eggs are a deep pink color.
3. Drain liquid from eggs. Arrange beets and onions on serving platter. Slice beets in half lengthwise and arrange on top of beets.

Tip
* The longer you let your eggs pickle in the refrigerator the more flavorful they will taste. Do not refrigerate for longer than 3 days.

Make Ahead
* *3 Days Ahead of Time:* The eggs can be hard-boiled and added to the pickling mixture up to 3 days ahead of time.

Breakfast

Classic Scrambled Eggs

Cheesy Scrambled Eggs with Chives

Perfect Eggs Benedict

Easy Eggs Florentine

Breakfast Bowl with Eggs and Chorizo

Simply Sensational Meaty Frittata

Creole Style Omelet

Huevos Rancheros

Poached Eggs and Havarti on Puff Pastry

Breakfast Parfait with Maple Hollandaise

Breakfast Sausage Poutine

Corn and Cheddar Enchiladas

California Turkey and Avocado Scramble

Breakfast Sausage and Eggs on Herb Flatbread

Corned Beef Hash with Poached Eggs

Spiced Quinoa Timbales with Poached Eggs

Egg Whites, Salmon and Capers on Pumpernickel

Latin American Poached Eggs With Chipotle Hollandaise

Sweet and Spicy Omelet Sandwich

Classic Scrambled Eggs

These classic scrambled eggs are foolproof in the egg cooker. This simple and tasty breakfast is even better with no fuss and easy cleanup.

Makes 1 Serving

	Non-stick cooking spray
2	eggs
2 tbsp	milk
	Kosher salt and freshly ground black pepper

1. Spray omelet bowl (tray) with non-stick cooking spray.
2. In a medium bowl, whisk together eggs and milk. Season with salt and pepper. Pour eggs into prepared omelet bowl. Fill water in the measuring container to the "Omelet/Poached" line and pour into the cooker. Transfer omelet bowl onto the boiling tray. Cover and press the Power button.
3. When the cooker beeps, transfer eggs to a serving plate. Serve immediately.

Tips
* For fluffier eggs, vigorously whisk eggs before adding to the cooker.
* For denser eggs, lightly whisk eggs before adding to the cooker.
* Serve with sausage links or bacon and toast.

Variations
* Add 2 tbsp grated pepper jack cheese to the eggs in step 1.
* Add 2 tbsp mild, medium or hot salsa with the eggs in step 1 and reduce the milk to 3 tbsp.

Cheesy Scrambled Eggs with Chives

A rich and creamy ricotta cheese gets interspersed with a bit of chives to make these scrambled eggs explode with flavor.

Makes 1 Serving

	Non-stick cooking spray
2	eggs
1/4 cup	whole milk ricotta
2 tbsp	minced chives or scallion greens
	Kosher salt and freshly ground black pepper

1. Spray omelet (poaching) bowl with non-stick cooking spray.
2. In a medium bowl, whisk together eggs, ricotta and chives. Season with salt and pepper. Pour eggs into prepared omelet bowl. Fill water in the measuring container to the "Omelet/Poached" line and pour into the cooker. Transfer omelet bowl onto the boiling tray. Cover and press the Power button.
3. When the cooker beeps, transfer eggs to a serving plate. Serve immediately.

Tips
* Do not over-whisk your eggs. The eggs will poof up while cooking and them cave in which causes them to be denser and not the ideal fluffy texture.

Perfect Eggs Benedict

There is nothing quite like the pure joy that is experienced with this delectable classic brunch dish. With the egg cooker poaching eggs is easy and foolproof.

Makes 2 Servings

Hollandaise

2	egg yolks
1 tbsp	lemon juice
1 tsp	Dijon mustard (optional)
6 tbsp	sticks unsalted butter, melted
	Kosher salt

Base Layers

	Non-stick cooking spray
2	eggs
1	English muffin, split in half
2	1/4-inch thick slices of Canadian bacon
	Hungarian paprika

1. *Hollandaise:* In the top of a double boiler or a heatproof bowl over simmering water, whisk the yolks, lemon juice and mustard until well combined. Drizzle in the butter, whisking continuously, and cook 1 to 2 minutes or until sauce has thickened. Season to taste with salt. Let the sauce stand in the bowl over simmering water, whisking occasionally, until ready to use.
2. *Base Layers:* Spray poaching tray with non-stick cooking spray. Add eggs to the poaching tray. Fill water in the measuring container to the "Omelet/Poached" line and pour into the cooker. Transfer poaching tray onto the boiling tray. Cover and press the Power button.
3. Meanwhile, toast muffin halves and transfer to serving plates. Set aside.
4. In a skillet over medium-high heat, add Canadian bacon and cook, turning once, about 1 minute per side until lightly browned and heated through. Transfer to the top of the muffin halves.
5. When the cooker beeps, transfer eggs to the top of each Canadian bacon slice. Drizzle each with about 1/4 cup of hollandaise sauce, or more to your liking. Garnish with paprika. Serve immediately.

(Continued on next page)

Perfect Eggs Benedict (continued)

When you just can't get enough of eggs benedict, here are variations of the traditional that you will want to try.

Each Variation Makes 2 Servings

* ***Sautéed Spinach and Prosciutto Benedict:*** For the base layer: heat 1 tbsp virgin olive oil in a medium skillet. Add 1 cup lightly packed baby spinach leaves and cook, tossing, 5 minutes or until wilted. Substitute 2 thin slices prosciutto for the Canadian bacon. Layer prosciutto and spinach on top of muffin before adding egg and hollandaise sauce.

* ***Portobello Eggs Benedict:*** Heat 1 tbsp virgin olive oil in a medium skillet. Add 4 sliced button mushroom, 2 quartered artichoke hearts (from can), drained, 1 sliced roasted red pepper and cook over medium heat, stirring, 5 minutes or until mushrooms are softened. Stir mixture into hollandaise sauce. Add 2 portobello mushrooms, top side up, to a foil-lined baking sheet. Brush with olive oil. Roast in a 400°F oven for 10 to 12 minutes or until slightly softened. Arrange mushrooms bottom side up on serving plates. Fill with each with the artichoke hollandaise mixture and a poached egg. Garnish with chopped chives.

* ***Asparagus Gruyere Prosciutto Benedict:*** Substitute 2 slices toasted sourdough bread for the English muffin. Sauté 6 asparagus spears and arrange 3 on each top of sourdough. Add 1 slice of gruyere to the top of each. Broil for 20 seconds of until cheese is melted. Arrange 2 slices of prosciutto next to the asparagus per benedict. Stir in 1-1/2 tbsp grated gruyere and 1-1/2 tbsp grated parmesan to hollandaise sauce, mixing well. Add poached egg each benedict. Drizzle with hollandaise sauce. Garnish with fresh thyme leaves.

Tips
* The hollandaise sauce is also delicious served over cooked asparagus.
* Add 1/2 cup asparagus pieces to the poaching tray. Fill water in the measuring container to the "Hard" line and pour into the cooker. Cover and cook. Serve with leftover hollandaise sauce.

Easy Eggs Florentine

Eggs Florentine is a wonderful and nutritious brunch or breakfast dish. With the combination of wilted spinach and eggs, this dish is also a delicious and satisfying lunch.

Makes 2 Servings

	Non-stick cooking spray
2	eggs
8 oz	spinach, stems trimmed
1 tsp	sunflower or virgin olive oil
1	English muffin, split in half
	Hollandaise sauce (see page 32)
	Freshly grated nutmeg
	Freshly ground black pepper

1. Spray omelet (poaching) bowl with non-stick cooking spray. Add eggs to the poaching tray. Fill water in the measuring container to the "Omelet/Poached" line and pour into the cooker. Transfer poaching tray onto the boiling tray. Cover and press the Power button.
2. Meanwhile, in a large skillet over medium-high heat, add the oil and heat until shimmering. Add the spinach and cook, tossing with tongs, 1 to 2 minutes or until wilted. Transfer spinach to a colander and using the back of a spoon, press out any remaining liquid. Return spinach to the skillet, cover, and keep warm.
3. Toast muffin halves and transfer to serving plates.
4. Arrange cooked spinach, evenly divided, over the muffins. When the cooker beeps, transfer poached eggs to the top of the spinach. Drizzle each with about 1/4 cup of hollandaise sauce, or more to your liking. Garnish with nutmeg and season with pepper. Serve immediately.

Tips
* You can lightly butter the English muffins after toasting if you desire.
* Serve with a side of fresh fruit.

Breakfast Bowl with Eggs and Chorizo

Wake up your taste buds with these hearty little breakfast bowls that are packed with spices for an invigorating and filling start to your day.

Makes 2 Servings

2	large eggs
	Non-stick cooking spray
2 tbsp	cooked and crumbled chorizo sausage
1/2 cup	frozen potatoes O'Brien, cooked (see tip below)
1 tbsp	pepper jack cheese
1/4	avocado, diced
2 tbsp	salsa (optional)
2 tbsp	sour cream

1. Spray omelet (poaching) bowl with non-stick cooking spray.
2. In a medium bowl, whisk eggs together. Stir in the sausage. Pour mixture into the omelet bowl. Fill water in the measuring container to the "Omelet/Poached" line and pour into the cooker. Transfer omelet bowl onto the boiling tray. Cover and press the Power button.
3. Meanwhile, divide the warm potatoes O'Brien between 2 serving bowls.
4. When the cooker beeps, layer 1/2 of the egg mixture, pepper jack cheese and avocado on top of the potatoes. Top with salsa (if using) and a dollop of sour cream. Serve immediately.

Tips
* Frozen Potatoes O'Brien come in 28 oz packages, or about 2-1/2 cups. Cook according to package directions.
* You can make the frozen potatoes ahead of time, cover and refrigerate. Reheat the potatoes in the microwave for 1 minute, just before using.
* Potatoes O'Brien are a fantastic side dish or casserole addition. Use leftover cooked potatoes in this recipe.

Simply Sensational Meaty Frittata

This simple frittata is so easy and quick to make and with custom fillings to suit your tastes it makes a great breakfast, lunch or dinner.

Makes 1 Serving

	Non-stick cooking spray
1/4 cup	cooked chopped spinach
2 tbsp	chopped pancetta
2	eggs
1 tbsp	minced onions
1 tsp	minced garlic
1/2 tsp	kosher salt
1/8 tsp	freshly ground black pepper
1 tbsp	shredded mozzarella cheese
	Chopped fresh tarragon (optional)

1. Spray omelet (poaching) bowl with non-stick cooking spray. Add spinach and pancetta to the prepared bowl.
2. In a medium bowl, lightly whisk together eggs, onions, garlic, salt and pepper. Pour eggs into the omelet bowl. Sprinkle with mozzarella cheese. Fill water in the measuring container to the "Omelet/Poached" line and pour into the cooker. Transfer omelet bowl onto the boiling tray. Cover and press the Power button.
3. When the cooker beeps, transfer eggs to a serving plate. Garnish with tarragon, if using. Serve immediately or for up to 1 hour at room temperature.

Tips

* The spinach and onions can be steamed in the omelet bowl of the egg cooker ahead of time, if you prefer. Fill water in the measuring container to the "Hard" line and pour into the cooker. Transfer omelet bowl onto the boiling tray. Cover and press the Power button. Continue with the recipe.
* Vegetables in the following variations can also be steamed before adding to the frittata. Follow the directions in the previous tip.

(Continued on next page)

Simply Sensational Meaty Frittata (continued)

Variations

* ***Ham and Broccoli****:* Omit the spinach, pancetta, garlic and mozzarella. Add 2 tbsp diced cooked ham, 1/4 cup diced cooked broccoli, 1 tsp ground mustard and 1 tbsp shredded cheddar.

* ***Smoked Trout and Asparagus:*** Omit the spinach, pancetta, garlic and mozzarella. Add 2 tbsp flaked smoked trout or salmon, 1/4 cup sliced cooked asparagus and 1-1/2 tbsp Parmigiano-Reggiano cheese.

* ***Tomato and Bacon:*** Omit the spinach, pancetta, garlic and mozzarella. Add 1/3 cup chopped plum tomatoes, 2 tbsp cooked and crumbled bacon, 1 tbsp shredded Swiss cheese and 2 tsp packed chopped fresh basil, reserving 1 tsp for garnish.

Creole Style Omelet

Spice up your omelets with these Creole seasonings that are a New Orleans favorite. With the influences of Spanish and French settlers, these flavors are truly unique.

Makes 2 Servings

4 tsp	half-and-half
2 tsp	creole seasoning
1/4 tsp	crushed red pepper flakes
2 tsp	virgin olive oil
1/2	sweet bell pepper, seeded and diced
1/4	sweet onion, such as Vidalia, diced
1 tsp	minced garlic
2 oz	cooked andouille sausage, coarsely chopped
2 oz	cooked small shrimp
	Non-stick cooking spray
4	large eggs

1. In a small bowl, whisk together, half-and-half, creole seasoning and red pepper flakes. Set aside.
2. In large skillet over medium heat, add oil and heat until shimmering. Add bell peppers and onion and cook, stirring, 3 to 5 minutes or until peppers and onion are softened. Add in garlic, sausage and shrimp and cook, stirring, 1 minute or until garlic is fragrant and sausage and shrimp are heated through. Add in half-and-half mixture and cook, stirring, 2 to 3 minutes or until slightly thickened. Cover, set aside and keep warm.
3. Spray omelet (poaching) bowl with non-stick cooking spray. In the small bowl, whisk eggs together. Pour 1/2 of the egg mixture into the omelet bowl. Fill water in the measuring container to the "Omelet/Poached" line and pour into the cooker. Transfer omelet bowl onto the boiling tray. Cover and press the Power button.
4. When the cooker beeps, spoon 1/2 of the sausage mixture onto one side of the eggs. Transfer omelet to serving plate, folding unfilled half over the top of the filling. Repeat with remaining eggs and sausage mixture. Serve immediately.

Huevos Rancheros

This classic Mexican breakfast is so easy to make in the egg cooker and there is no fussing or mess with additional pots and pans. Even better, the flavors are delightful.

Makes 1 Serving

	Non-stick cooking spray
2 tbsp	salsa
1	egg
1	corn or flour tortilla (about 6-inch diameter), warmed
1 tbsp	shredded cotija or Mexican cheese blend
2 tsp	chopped fresh cilantro (optional)

1. Spray 1 side of poaching tray with non-stick cooking spray. Add egg to the sprayed side of the tray and the salsa in the other side of the tray. Fill water in the measuring container to the "Omelet/Poached" line and pour into the cooker. Transfer poaching tray onto the boiling tray. Cover and press the Power button.
2. Place warmed tortilla on serving plate. When the cooker beeps, transfer egg to the top of the tortilla. Pour salsa around the egg. Sprinkle with cheese. Garnish with cilantro, if using.

Tip
* To heat the tortillas, wrap them in paper towels and microwave for 40 to 50 seconds. You can also heat the tortillas in a non-stick skillet over medium-high heat, turning once, for 30 seconds per side or until warm.

Variations
* For a smokier chile flavor, add 1 tbsp chopped chipotle chiles in adobo sauce (with sauce) and reduce the salsa to 1 tbsp.
* Add 2 tsp thinly sliced green onions as a garnish.

Poached Eggs and Havarti on Puff Pastry

Elegant puff pastry shells are filled with buttery havarti cheese and then topped with a perfectly poached egg and crumbled bacon.

Makes 2 Servings

2	frozen puff pastry shells, baked (see tip below)
1/2 cup	shredded havarti cheese
	Non-stick cooking spray
2	eggs
	Kosher salt and freshly ground pepper
2	slices bacon, cooked and crumbled
	Chopped fresh chives

1. Sprinkle havarti into the center of each warm puff pastry shell.
2. Spray poaching tray with non-stick cooking spray. Add eggs to the poaching tray. Fill water in the measuring container to the "Omelet/Poached" line and pour into the cooker. Transfer poaching tray onto the boiling tray. Cover and press the Power button.
3. When the cooker beeps, transfer poached eggs to the top of the cheese in the puff pastry shell. Season to taste with salt and pepper. Sprinkle with bacon and garnish with chives.

Tips
* 1 package (10 oz) frozen pastry shells contain 6 shells. Remove 2 shells and keep the remaining shells frozen for another use. Prepare shells according to package directions.
* You can use puff pastry sheets if you choose. Arrange sheets in cupcake pans. Prepare according to package directions.

Breakfast Parfait with Maple Hollandaise

Layers upon layers of eggs, bacon, ham, cheddar cheese and a maple syrup hollandaise sauce imbue this parfait with heavenly flavors.

Makes 2 Servings

Two 6 oz microwave-safe parfait glasses

2	egg yolks
2 tbsp	pure maple syrup
1 tbsp	lemon juice
1/2 tsp	ground mustard
Pinch	cayenne pepper
6 tbsp	sticks unsalted butter, melted
	Kosher salt
2	eggs
2	slices bacon, cooked and chopped
2/3 cup	diced ham
6 tbsp	shredded cheddar cheese
4 tbsp	diced tomatoes
4 tbsp	diced avocado

1. In the top of a double boiler or a heatproof bowl over simmering water, whisk the yolks, maple syrup, lemon juice, mustard and cayenne until well combined. Drizzle in the butter, whisking continuously, and cook 1 to 2 minutes or until sauce has thickened. Season to taste with salt. Let the sauce stand in the bowl over simmering water, whisking occasionally, until ready to use.
2. In a medium bowl, whisk eggs together. Pour mixture into the omelet bowl. Fill water in the measuring container to the "Omelet/Poached" line and pour into the cooker. Transfer omelet bowl onto the boiling tray. Cover and press the Power button. Cool.
3. In each parfait glass, layer 3 tbsp scrambled eggs, 2 tbsp hollandaise, 1/2 bacon, 3 tbsp scrambled eggs, 2 tbsp hollandaise, 1/3 cup ham, 2 tbsp scrambled eggs, 2 tbsp Maple Hollandaise and 3 tbsp cheddar cheese. Cover and microwave on high for 1 minute, or until heated through. Garnish with tomatoes and avocadoes. Serve immediately.

Breakfast Sausage Poutine

See for yourself if this French fries, cheese curd, egg and gravy dish isn't the messiest, chin dripping and engaging dish you've ever dove in to.

Makes 2 Servings

Pepper Cream Gravy

2 tsp	butter or bacon drippings
2 tsp	all-purpose flour
1 cup	milk
2 tsp	heavy cream
1⁄4 tsp	kosher salt
1⁄4 tsp	freshly ground black pepper

French fry layers

1 tsp	butter
1⁄4 lb	button mushrooms, sliced
3 oz	cooked ground turkey sausage
1/2 lb	frozen French fried potatoes
4	eggs
3 oz	cheese curds

1. *Pepper-Cream Gravy:* In a small saucepan over medium heat, melt the butter. Slowly whisk in the flour and cook, stirring, 1 minute or until golden. Whisk in milk, cream, salt and pepper and cook, stirring, 5 minutes or until thickened. Remove from heat; cover and keep warm.
2. In a medium sauté pan, melt butter over medium high heat. Add mushrooms and sauté, stirring frequently, 5 to 7 minutes or until softened. Add sausage and cook, stirring, 1 minute or until warm.
3. In a medium bowl, whisk eggs together. Pour 1/2 mixture into the omelet bowl. Fill water in the measuring container to the "Omelet/Poached" line and pour into the cooker. Transfer omelet bowl onto the boiling tray. Cover and press the Power button. When cooker beeps, remove eggs. Repeat with remaining eggs.
4. Meanwhile, cook French fries according to package instructions. Transfer fries to serving bowls.
5. Arrange 1/2 mushroom sausage mixture and cheese curds over the top of each bowl. Bake for 2 to 3 minutes, or until cheese is softened. Top with scrambled eggs and gravy. Serve warm.

Corn and Cheddar Enchiladas

Make this simple and flavorful enchilada dish for weekend guests. The enchiladas are easily refrigerated or frozen, if you have leftovers, or if you'd just like to have a quick and ready-to-eat breakfast or lunch during the week.

Makes 8 Servings

13-by 9-inch baking dish, lightly greased
Preheat oven to 350°F

8	eggs
1	can (8 oz) cream-style corn
2/3 cup	shredded cheddar cheese
1	can (4 oz) chopped green chilies
2 tsp	ground taco seasoning
1/4 tsp	kosher salt
8	corn tortillas warmed
1	bottle (8 oz) mild taco sauce
	Sour cream (optional)

1. Pierce the bottom of each egg. Fill water in the measuring container to the "Hard" line and pour into the cooker. Place the eggs in the boiling tray bottom-side up. Cover and press the Power button. When the cooker beeps, transfer eggs to a bowl of cold water until cool enough to handle. Peel eggs under cold running water; dry with a paper towel. Coarsely chop eggs.
2. In a medium bowl, add the eggs, corn, cheese, green chilies, taco seasoning and salt.
3. Place 1 tortilla on a plate and spoon 1/2 cup of the egg filling down the center of the tortilla. Roll up the tortilla, folding in the ends as you go. Place rolled tortillas seam side down in prepared baking dish. Drizzle with taco sauce. Bake, uncovered, for 15 minutes or until heated through. Serve warm with a dollop of sour cream, if using.

Tip
* Roll individual enchiladas in foil, sealing tightly. Refrigerate for up to 5 days or freeze for up to 3 months. Reheat before serving.

California Turkey and Avocado Scramble

In this hearty breakfast dish, herb roasted red potatoes are topped with eggs scrambled with smoked turkey, avocado and Monterey jack cheese. This dish then gets smothered in ranchero sauce.

Makes 2 Servings

Baking sheet, covered with foil and sprayed with non-stick cooking spray

1 lb	small red potatoes, quartered
1 tsp	chopped garlic
1 tsp	fresh rosemary, chopped
1 tsp	fresh thyme, chopped
2 tsp	virgin olive oil
4	eggs
1/4 lb	smoked turkey breast, cubed
1	avocado, peeled, pitted and cubes
2 tbsp	shredded Monterey jack cheese
	Ranchero Sauce (mild, medium, or hot)
	Cilantro leaves (optional)

1. In a large bowl, toss potatoes with garlic, rosemary, thyme and oil, until potatoes are well coated. Arrange on prepared baking sheet. Roast, tossing occasionally, for 45 minutes or until fork-tender.
2. Meanwhile, spray omelet bowl with non-stick cooking spray. In a medium bowl, whisk eggs together. Stir in turkey and avocado. Pour 1/2 mixture into the omelet bowl. Fill water in the measuring container to the "Omelet/Poached" line and pour into the cooker. Transfer omelet bowl onto the boiling tray. Cover and press the Power button. When cooker beeps, remove eggs. Repeat with remaining egg mixture.
3. Arrange potatoes on serving plates. Top with scrambled eggs and ranchero sauce. Garnish with cilantro, if using.

Tip
* Use pepper jack cheese in place of the Monterey jack to spice up your dish.

Breakfast Sausage and Eggs on Herb Flatbread

This recipe starts with a wonderfully flavored herb flatbread, then we smother it with tomato sauce, cheese and scrambled eggs and top it off with arugula.

Makes 2 Servings

1 baking sheet sprayed with non-stick cooking spray

2	prepared flatbread crusts (individual serving size)
1 tbsp	virgin olive oil
1 tsp	dried basil leaves
1/2 tsp	crushed dried rosemary leaves
1 tsp	minced garlic
1/4 lb	ground breakfast sausage, cooked
1/4	small onion, diced
1/3 cup	tomato sauce
1/3 cup	shredded sharp cheddar cheese
4 tsp	shredded Parmesan cheese
2	eggs
2 tbsp	lightly packed arugula
1 tsp	lime zest
	Freshly ground black pepper

1. Preheat oven to 375°F. Arrange flatbread crusts on prepared baking sheet.
2. In small bowl, combine oil, basil, rosemary and garlic, mixing well. Brush mixture over dough. Sprinkle sausage and onions over the top. Drizzle with tomato sauce. Bake for 5 to 10 minutes or until crust is golden brown and heated through. Remove from oven, sprinkle with cheddar and parmesan cheese. Keep warm.
3. Meanwhile, spray poaching tray with non-stick cooking spray. Add eggs to the poaching tray. Fill water in the measuring container to the "Omelet/Poached" line and pour into the cooker. Transfer poaching tray onto the boiling tray. Cover and press the Power button.
4. When the cooker beeps, transfer eggs to top of flatbread slices. Garnish with arugula and lime zest. Season to taste with pepper.

Corned Beef Hash with Poached Eggs

This hearty, wild west style breakfast dish will satisfy even the heartiest of eaters. You may even want to try this dish as breakfast for dinner!

Makes 2 Servings

1 tbsp	vegetable oil
4 oz	cooked corned beef, chopped
1 cup	frozen potatoes O'Brien
1 tbsp	chopped fresh chives
1 tbsp	chopped fresh thyme
2	eggs
2	slices cheddar cheese
	Kosher salt and freshly ground black pepper

1. In a medium skillet, heat the oil over medium-high heat until shimmering. Add the corned beef and cook, stirring, 3 minutes or until lightly browned. Stir in the potatoes and cook, without stirring, 6 minutes or until brown and crisp on the bottom. Add thyme and cook, turning occasionally, 15 minutes or until evenly browned. Transfer hash to serving bowls and add a slice of cheese. Keep warm.
2. Meanwhile, spray poaching tray with non-stick cooking spray. Add eggs to the poaching tray. Fill water in the measuring container to the "Omelet/Poached" line and pour into the cooker. Transfer poaching tray onto the boiling tray. Cover and press the Power button.
3. When the cooker beeps, transfer eggs to top of hash and cheese. Season to taste with salt and pepper.

Tip

* In place of the frozen potatoes O'Brien, you can combine 1/2 onion (chopped), 1/2 bell pepper (chopped) and 1 baking potato (peeled and shredded) in a small bowl.

Spiced Quinoa Timbales with Poached Eggs

This protein-packed breakfast is infused with a bounty of spices, tomatoes and raisins and is a great way to start your day.

Makes 2 Servings

Two 3/4 cup timbale molds or ramekins, lightly greased

1/4 cup	minced onion
1 tsp	virgin olive oil
1/2 tsp	ground cumin
Pinch	ground cinnamon
Pinch	ground turmeric
1/3 cup	quinoa, rinsed and drained
1/3 cup	chicken broth
3 tbsp	water
2 tbsp	dried raisins
3	cherry tomatoes, chopped
Pinch	kosher salt
2	eggs
	Chopped fresh parsley

1. In a small saucepan, over medium heat, add the oil and heat until shimmering. Add the onion and cook, stirring, 3 minutes or until softened. Add the cumin, cinnamon and turmeric and cook, stirring, for 30 seconds. Add the quinoa and cook, stirring, for 1 minute or until fragrant. Add the broth, water, raisins, tomatoes and salt and simmer, covered, for 8 minutes or until the liquid is absorbed. Remove from heat and let stand, covered, 5 minutes.
2. Meanwhile, spray poaching tray with non-stick cooking spray. Add eggs to the poaching tray. Fill water in the measuring container to the "Omelet/Poached" line and pour into the cooker. Transfer poaching tray onto the boiling tray. Cover and press the Power button.
3. When the cooker beeps, open cover. Stir parsley into quinoa and spoon into timbale molds and pack lightly. Invert timbales onto serving plates. Transfer eggs to top of timbales and serve warm.

Egg Whites, Salmon and Capers on Pumpernickel

This light, open-face breakfast sandwich has a wonderful savory combination of salmon, tomatoes and capers served over a toasted pumpernickel slice.

Makes 1 Serving

2	egg whites
1 tbsp	finely chopped red onions
1/2 tsp	capers
Pinch	kosher salt
1	slice pumpernickel or rye bread
1	slice tomato
1 oz	thinly sliced smoked salmon
	Freshly ground black pepper

1. Spray omelet bowl with non-stick cooking spray. In a small bowl, whisk eggs together. Stir in onions, capers and salt. Pour mixture into the omelet bowl. Fill water in the measuring container to the "Omelet/Poached" line and pour into the cooker. Transfer omelet bowl onto the boiling tray. Cover and press the Power button.
2. Meanwhile, toast pumpernickel bread. Transfer to a serving plate. When cooker beeps, transfer eggs to top of bread. Layer with tomato and smoked salmon. Season to taste with pepper.

Tips
* Leftover egg yolks can be refrigerated in an airtight container for up to 3 days.
* You can use the whole egg in this recipe if you prefer.

Latin American Eggs with Chipotle Hollandaise

A zesty hollandaise sauce tops toasted corn arepas, bacon and poached eggs. This is a great-tasting dish to add variety to your mornings.

Makes 2 Servings

Hollandaise

2	egg yolks
1 tbsp	lemon juice
1/2 tbsp	sauce from jar of chipotle chiles in adobo sauce
6 tbsp	sticks unsalted butter, melted
	Kosher salt

Base Layers

	Non-stick cooking spray
2	eggs
2	white corn arepas
2	1/4-inch thick slices of Canadian bacon
	Paprika

1. *Hollandaise:* In the top of a double boiler or a heatproof bowl over simmering water, whisk the yolks, lemon juice and adobo sauce until well combined. Drizzle in the butter, whisking continuously, and cook 1 to 2 minutes or until sauce has thickened. Season to taste with salt. Let the sauce stand in the bowl over simmering water, whisking occasionally, until ready to use.
2. *Base Layers:* Spray poaching tray with non-stick cooking spray. Add eggs to the poaching tray. Fill water in the measuring container to the "Omelet/Poached" line and pour into the cooker. Transfer poaching tray onto the boiling tray. Cover and press the Power button.
3. Meanwhile, in a medium skillet over medium-high heat, add the arepas and heat, turning once, 10 to 15 seconds per side or until warmed through. Transfer to a serving plate. In the same skillet add the Canadian bacon and cook, turning once, about 1 minute per side until lightly browned and heated through. Transfer to the top of the arepas.
4. When the cooker beeps, transfer eggs to the top of each Canadian bacon slice. Drizzle with hollandaise sauce. Garnish with paprika. Serve immediately.

Sweet and Spicy Omelet Sandwich

The contrasting flavors of a spicy pork sausage, cheddar cheese and sweet cinnamon raisin bread, spread with maple syrup butter, make this omelet sandwich a scrumptious breakfast treat.

Makes 1 Serving

	Non-stick cooking spray
2	eggs
1	pork sausage patty, cooked
2 tsp	butter, softened
1 tsp	pure maple syrup
2	slices cinnamon raisin bread
1	slice cheddar cheese
	Kosher salt and freshly ground black pepper

1. Spray omelet bowl with non-stick cooking spray. In a small bowl, whisk eggs. Pour mixture into the omelet bowl. Fill water in the measuring container to the "Omelet/Poached" line and pour into the cooker. Transfer omelet bowl onto the boiling tray. Cover and press the Power button.

2. Meanwhile, in a small bowl, combine butter and maple syrup, mixing well. Toast cinnamon raisin bread. Spread mixture on 1 side of each slice of bread. Transfer to a serving plate, spread side up. Add cheese and sausage to the top of one slice. When cooker beeps, transfer eggs to top of the sausage patty. Place the other bread slice, spread side down, on top of the eggs. Serve immediately.

Tip

* I prefer using a sharp cheddar cheese in this recipe because it adds a nice contrast in flavors. However, any type of cheddar cheese will work.

Main Dishes and Sides

Pepperoni and Egg Mini Pizzas

Pecan and Grape Chicken Salad

Bacon Egg Lettuce and Tomato Sandwich

Turkey Club Flatbread Sandwich

Zesty Pulled Pork and Avocado Burrito

Spanish Club Sandwich

Cajun Shrimp Tacos with Chipotle Crema

Sliced Ham, Eggs and Avocado Torta

Quick and Easy Potato Salad for Two

Eggs Rockefeller

Chipotle Roasted Chicken and Egg Burrito

Pancetta, Chard and Poached Eggs With Zucchini Fettucine

Green Bean, Tuna, Tomato and Quinoa Salad

Mixed Greens with Rosemary Beets and Dijon Mint Dressing

Refreshing Egg Salad

Poached Eggs with Artichokes Provençal

Egg Salad Banh Mi

Cobb Salad With Garlic Dijon Vinaigrette

Chunky Deli Potato Salad

Hearty Ham, Cheddar and Asparagus Bake

Zesty Hash Brown, Bacon and Egg Strata

Egg Filled Ham and Cheese Corn Muffins

Pepperoni and Egg Mini Pizzas

These little pizzas make the perfect after school snack, a quick an easy lunch or a late-night movie snack. Ready-made pizza crusts get topped with diced pepperoni, pizza sauce, hard-boiled eggs and gooey cheese.

Makes 4 Servings

Egg Cooker
Baking Sheet Lined with Foil

2	eggs
4	4-inch ready-made-pizza crusts, toasted
1/2 cup	pizza sauce
1/4 cup	diced pepperoni
1/2 cup	grated mozzarella
	Crushed red pepper flakes (optional)
	Grated parmesan (optional)

1. Pierce the bottom of each egg. Fill water in the measuring container to the "Hard" line and pour into the cooker. Place the eggs in the boiling tray bottom-side up. Cover and press the Power button. When the cooker beeps, transfer eggs to a bowl of cold water until cool enough to handle. Peel eggs under cold running water; dry with a paper towel. Slice eggs crosswise.
2. Meanwhile, preheat broiler with top oven rack 4 inches from heat.
3. Arrange pizza crusts on baking sheet. Spread each crust with equal amounts of pizza sauce. Arrange egg slices on top of sauce. Sprinkle with pepperoni and mozzarella, evenly divided, on top of eggs.
4. Broil 3 to 5 minutes or until cheese is melted. Garnish with pepper flakes and parmesan, if using. Serve warm.

Variation
* Look for ready-made pizza crusts in the Italian or bakery section of your grocery store.
* If you are not able to find small pizza crusts, you can use a large ready-made crust and cut it into 4-inch round pieces using a cookie cutter or a kitchen scissors.

Pecan and Grape Chicken Salad

One of my favorite delis has a chicken salad similar to this one. I have modified it to include more protein from the hard-boiled eggs and added for few other twists to make the flavor explode.

Makes 8 Servings

4 cups	shredded rotisserie chicken or leftover roasted chicken
1-1/2 cups	seedless green grapes, halved
1 cup	chopped celery
3/4 cup	sliced green onions, white part only
4	eggs
1/2 cup	real mayonnaise
1/4 cup	sour cream
1 tbsp	prepared mustard
1 tsp	kosher salt
1/2 tsp	freshly ground black pepper
1/2 tsp	onion powder
1/2 tsp	ground paprika
1/2 cup	slivered pecans

1. Pierce the bottom of each egg. Fill water in the measuring container to the "Hard" line and pour into the cooker. Place the eggs in the boiling tray bottom-side up. Cover and press the Power button. When the cooker beeps, transfer eggs to a bowl of cold water until cool enough to handle. Peel eggs under cold running water; dry with a paper towel. Coarsely chop eggs.
2. In a large bowl, combine chicken, grapes, celery, onions and eggs. Set aside.
3. In a medium bowl, combine mayonnaise, mustard, salt, pepper, onion powder and paprika, mixing well. Pour mixture over the chicken mixture and stir gently to combine. Stir in almonds just before serving.

Make Ahead
* *3 Days Ahead of Time:* The chicken salad can be made ahead of time, stored in an airtight container and refrigerated for up to 3 days. Add the almonds just before serving.

Bacon Egg Lettuce and Tomato Sandwich

In this recipe, the classic BLT gets a protein and flavor boost with slices of hard-boiled eggs.

Makes 1 Serving

1	egg
2	slices hearty whole grain bread, toasted
1-1/2 tbsp	real mayonnaise
1/3 cup	lightly packed arugula
2	thick slices Applewood smoke bacon, cooked
1	roma tomato, sliced

1. Pierce the bottom of each egg. Fill water in the measuring container to the "Hard" line and pour into the cooker. Place the eggs in the boiling tray bottom-side up. Cover and press the Power button. When the cooker beeps, transfer eggs to a bowl of cold water until cool enough to handle. Peel eggs under cold running water; dry with a paper towel. Cut into slices.
2. Spread each slice of bread with mayonnaise. Layer one slice of bread, spread side up, with 1/2 of the arugula, 2 slices bacon, sliced eggs, tomatoes and top with remaining arugula. Top with remaining bread slice, spread side down. Serve.

Variations
* Substitute pita bread for the whole grain bread. Cut a slit in the pita to make a pocket. Spread mayonnaise inside pocket and fill with remaining ingredients.
* Omit the bacon and add in 1/2 avocado, peeled, pitted and slice to the sandwich.

Turkey Club Flatbread Sandwich

I love the combination of ham, turkey and cheese topped with a seasoned omelet inside this grilled flatbread sandwich.

Makes 1 Serving

	Non-stick cooking spray
2	eggs
1/4 tsp	ground thyme
1/4 tsp	onion powder
Pinch	freshly ground black pepper
1	flatbread (round or oblong)
1	slice deli ham
1	slice deli turkey
2 tbsp	shredded cheddar cheese
1	green onion, thinly sliced

1. Spray omelet bowl with non-stick cooking spray. In a small bowl, whisk eggs, thyme onion powder and black pepper together. Pour mixture into the omelet bowl. Fill water in the measuring container to the "Omelet/Poached" line and pour into the cooker. Transfer omelet bowl onto the boiling tray. Cover and press the Power button.
2. Meanwhile, on one half of the flatbread layer ham and turkey slices. When cooker beeps, transfer omelet to the top of the turkey. Sprinkle with cheese and onions. Fold flatbread in half. Transfer sandwich to a medium skillet over medium heat and cook, turning once, 2 to 3 minutes or until heated through.

Tips
* In place of the skillet, you can use a preheated panini press and cook 2 to 3 minutes, without turning.
* You can substitute an 8-inch tortilla for the flatbread.

Zesty Pulled Pork and Avocado Burrito

Just the right amount of spiciness paired with creamy avocado makes this pork burrito a go-to favorite.

Makes 1 Serving

	Non-stick cooking spray
2	eggs
1/4 cup	salsa
1	chipotle chili in adobo sauce, minced
1 tbsp	diced green chilies (from canned)
1	flour tortilla (10-inch), warmed
1/4 cup	pre-cooked pulled pork
1	small roma tomato, diced
1/2	avocado, cubed
1 tbsp	shredded Monterey Jack cheese

1. Spray omelet bowl with non-stick cooking spray. In a small bowl, whisk eggs. Pour mixture into the omelet bowl. Fill water in the measuring container to the "Omelet/Poached" line and pour into the cooker. Transfer omelet bowl onto the boiling tray. Cover and press the Power button.
2. Meanwhile, in a small bowl combine salsa, chipotle chili and green chilies, mixing well. Set aside.
3. When the cooker beeps, using a plastic spoon, spoon small chunks of the eggs onto the center of the tortilla in an oblong shape. Arrange pork, tomatoes, 1 tbsp salsa mixture, avocado and cheese on top of eggs. Roll up tortilla, folding in edges as you roll. Transfer tortilla, seam side down to serving plate. Serving with remaining salsa.

Tip
* Pre-cooked pulled pork can be found in the packaged meat section of your grocery store. Any leftover pork can be refrigerated in an airtight container up to 5 days.
* Use leftover pulled pork in sandwiches with your favorite BBQ sauce.
* Place a sheet or parchment paper under the tortilla before assembling. When tortilla has been rolled up, wrap tortilla in parchment paper for a burrito to go.

Spanish Club Sandwich

An exquisite combination of serrano ham, manchego cheese, sweet peppers and a zesty mayonnaise give this egg sandwich a unique twist.

Makes 2 Servings

3 tbsp	real mayonnaise
1-1/2 tbsp	chopped parsley
1 tsp	ground cumin
	Non-stick cooking spray
2	eggs
2	ciabatta rolls
4	thin slices serrano ham
2	slices manchego cheese
1	medium tomato, sliced
2	sweet peppers, seeded and julienned
2	romaine or iceberg lettuce leaves

1. Spray omelet bowl with non-stick cooking spray. In a small bowl, whisk eggs. Pour mixture into the omelet bowl. Fill water in the measuring container to the "Omelet/Poached" line and pour into the cooker. Transfer omelet bowl onto the boiling tray. Cover and press the Power button.
2. Meanwhile, in a small bowl, combine mayonnaise, parsley and cumin, mixing well. Slice ciabatta rolls in half horizontally. Spread mixture on cut side of each roll. Layer bottom of each roll with 1/2 each of the ham, cheese, tomato and peppers.
3. When the cooker beeps, using a plastic spoon, spoon small chunks of the eggs onto each of the sandwich layers. Top each with lettuce and cover with the top roll, spread side down. Serve.

Tip
* This sandwich can be wrapped and refrigerated for up to 1 day. Make it ahead of time and take it with you for lunch!

Cajun Shrimp Tacos with Chipotle Crema

This recipe pairs spicy shrimp with avocado, green onions and a zesty cream sauce that is then wrapped in tortillas for a full-flavored meal that will have you coming back for more.

Makes 2 Servings

1/4 cup	small (51/60) deveined shrimp
1/2 tsp	Cajun seasoning
1 tbsp	diced red onion
2	corn or flour tortillas
1/2	avocado, peeled, pitted and diced
1/4 cup	diced green onions, white and light green parts only
1/2 cup	Greek yogurt
1	chipotle in adobo sauce, diced
1 tsp	minced garlic
2 tsp	lime juice
	Kosher salt

1. In a small bowl, combine shrimp and Cajun seasoning, mixing well. Transfer to the omelet (poaching) bowl. Fill water in the measuring container to the "Hard" line and pour into the cooker. Transfer omelet bowl onto the boiling tray. Cover and press the Power button. When the cooker beeps, remove shrimp. Set aside.
2. Meanwhile, in a small bowl, combine, yogurt, chipotles, garlic and lime juice, mixing well. Season with salt.
3. Arrange shrimp in the middle of the tortillas. Top with avocado, onions and tomatoes (if using). Drizzle with chipotle crema. Roll up tortillas. Serve immediately.

Sliced Ham, Eggs and Avocado Torta

The torta is one of Mexico's fabulous stuffed sandwiches that is a wonderful meal for anytime of the day. This version is packed with sliced ham, eggs, cheese, tomatoes, avocados and chin-dripping goodness.

Makes 1 Serving

	Non-stick cooking spray
2	eggs
1/4 cup	queso fresco
1 tbsp	chopped cilantro
1	torta roll or ciabatta roll, sliced horizontally
1 tbsp	real mayonnaise
2	slices deli-style ham
1/2	avocado, sliced
	Freshly ground black pepper
2	thin slices tomato
1	thin slice red onion, rings separated

1. Spray omelet bowl with non-stick cooking spray. In a small bowl, whisk eggs. Pour mixture into the omelet bowl. Fill water in the measuring container to the "Omelet/Poached" line and pour into the cooker. Transfer omelet bowl onto the boiling tray. Cover and press the Power button.
2. In another small bowl, crumble the queso fresco and add the cilantro, mixing well. Set aside.
3. Spread bottom cut side of torta roll with mayonnaise. Layer ham and avocado slices on top.
4. When the cooker beeps, transfer the eggs to the top of the avocado. Season to taste with pepper. Add the tomato and onion slices. Sprinkle with the queso mixture. Cover with the top roll, spread side down. Serve immediately.

Tip
* This sandwich works equally well with 2 sliced hard-boiled eggs in place of the scrambled eggs.
* You can substitute the queso fresco with cotija or a mild feta.

Quick and Easy Potato Salad for Two

When you want have a craving for potato salad and don't want to make the crowd size version, you have the perfect solution with this tangy and tasty recipe.

Makes 2 Servings

4	small red potatoes
2	eggs
1/2	small celery rib, chopped
1/4 cup	Greek yogurt
2 tbsp	pickle relish
1 tsp	ground mustard
1/4 tsp	onion powder
1/4 tsp	kosher salt

1. Pierce the bottom of the eggs. Using a fork, poke the potatoes all over. Fill water in the measuring container to the "Hard" line and pour into the cooker. Place the eggs in the boiling tray bottom-side up. Place the potatoes in the cooker with the eggs. Cover and press the Power button. When the cooker beeps, transfer eggs and potatoes to a bowl of cold water until cool enough to handle. Peel eggs under cold running water; dry with a paper towel. Chop eggs and potatoes. Transfer to a medium bowl and add celery.
2. Meanwhile, combine yogurt, relish, mustard, onion powder and salt, mixing well. Add mixture to potatoes, mixing well to combine. Serve immediately.

Tip
* Potato salad can be refrigerated in an airtight container for up to 3 days.

Eggs Rockefeller

Poached eggs replace oysters in this take-off from the traditional dish. Spinach is paired with Applewood smoked bacon and cooked in a delightfully creamy sauce and then topped with a perfectly poached egg.

Makes 2 Servings

1/4 lb	Applewood smoked bacon
1/4	sweet onion, finely diced
1/2 tsp	minced garlic
1/3 lb	baby spinach leaves
1/3 cup	heavy cream
3 tbsp	grated parmesan cheese
	Kosher salt and freshly ground black pepper
3 tbsp	bread crumbs
	Non-stick cooking spray
4	eggs

1. In a medium skillet over medium heat, cook bacon until crisp. Transfer bacon to a paper towel lined plate. Crumble bacon when cool. Pour off all but 1 tbsp drippings from skillet and return to heat.

2. Add onions to the skillet and cook, stirring, 3 to 4 minutes or until softened. Add garlic and spinach and cook, stirring, 1 to 2 minutes or until garlic is fragrant and spinach is wilted. Return bacon to the skillet. Reduce heat to medium-low, stir in cream and bring to a simmer. Cook, stirring, 2 to 3 minutes or until cream has thickened. Stir in parmesan. Season to taste with salt and pepper, mixing to combine. Divide mixture between ramekins or oven-proof bowls. Sprinkle each with 1-1/2 tbsp bread crumbs.

3. Meanwhile, spray poaching tray with non-stick cooking spray. Add eggs to the poaching tray. Fill water in the measuring container to the "Omelet/Poached" line and pour into the cooker. Transfer poaching tray onto the boiling tray. Cover and press the Power button. When the cooker beeps, transfer eggs to a bowl of warm water to keep warm. Repeat with remaining 2 eggs.

4. Meanwhile, preheat broiler. Arrange 2 eggs to top of each spinach filled ramekin. Broil until crumbs are browned. Serve immediately.

Chipotle Roasted Chicken and Egg Burrito

This burrito is so easy to make using leftover rotisserie chicken and infused with flavor from the chipotle and green chiles, salsa and avocadoes that you may have just found a new favorite go-to dish.

Makes 1 Serving

	Non-stick cooking spray
2	eggs
1/4 cup	salsa verde
1/4 cup	diced avocado
2 tsp	minced chili in adobo sauce
1	flour tortilla (10 inch diameter), warmed
1/4 cup	shredded rotisserie chicken (dark or white meat or a combination)
1/2	roma tomato, chopped
1 tbsp	canned diced green chilies
2 tbsp	Monterey jack cheese
	Cilantro leaves (optional)

1. Spray omelet bowl with non-stick cooking spray. In a small bowl, whisk eggs. Pour mixture into the omelet bowl. Fill water in the measuring container to the "Omelet/Poached" line and pour into the cooker. Transfer omelet bowl onto the boiling tray. Cover and press the Power button.
2. Meanwhile, in a small bowl, combine salsa, avocado, chilies in adobo sauce, mixing well. Set aside
3. When the cooker beeps, transfer eggs to center of tortilla. Arrange chicken, tomatoes, chilies and cheese on top of eggs. Roll up tortilla, folding in sides as you roll.
4. Serve immediately with prepared salsa on the side. Garnish with cilantro leaves, if using.

Tip
* Any leftover roasted chicken you have on hand will work in place of the rotisserie chicken.
* Substitute pulled cooked pork shoulder for the shredded chicken.

Pancetta, Chard and Poached Eggs With Zucchini Fettucine

This is a delightful way to get a boost of vegetables and protein into your daily diet with this light and fabulous combination of fall vegetables.

Makes 2 Servings

Spiralizer or box grater

	Non-stick cooking spray
2	eggs
1/4 cup	diced pancetta
2	Swiss chard leaves, torn
2 tsp	butter
2	medium zucchini, ends trimmed and spiralized (see Tip below)
	Kosher salt and freshly ground black pepper
	Grated parmesan cheese

1. Spray poaching tray with non-stick cooking spray. Add eggs to the poaching tray. Fill water in the measuring container to the "Omelet/Poached" line and pour into the cooker. Transfer poaching tray onto the boiling tray. Cover and press the Power button.
2. Meanwhile, in a large skillet over medium heat, sauté the pancetta, stirring occasionally, 5 minutes or until crispy. Using a slotted spoon, transfer pancetta to a paper towel-lined plate. Discard all but 2 tsp of the grease from the skillet. Add Swiss chard and cook, tossing gently, 5 minutes or until tender. Transfer chard to the plate with the pancetta.
3. In the same skillet, heat butter until melted. Add the zucchini and cook, gently tossing, 2 minutes or until slightly tender. Add in chard and pancetta and cook, stirring, 1 minute or until zucchini is done to your liking and mixture is warmed through. Season to taste with salt and pepper. Transfer to serving bowls. When the cooker beeps, transfer 1 poached egg to the top of each serving. Sprinkle with parmesan. Serve.

Tip
* Using a spiralizer or a box grater, cut zucchini into medium-wide strands.

Green Bean, Tuna, Tomato and Quinoa Salad

This riff on the classic salad niçoise takes advantage of quinoa in place of the more traditional potatoes for a delectable departure from the standard.

Makes 4 Servings

8 oz	French green beans, trimmed
4	eggs
1/4 cup	white wine vinegar
1/2	shallot, minced
1 tbsp	Dijon mustard
1 tsp	kosher salt
1/4 tsp	freshly ground black pepper
6 tbsp	extra virgin olive oil
1/4 cup	loosely packed fresh parsley leaves
4	Boston lettuce leaves
2 cups	cooked quinoa, cooled
8 oz	cherry tomatoes, halved
6	sun-dried tomatoes in oil, thinly sliced (about 1/8-inch)
1/2 cup	Kalamata or niçoise olives
2	cans (4.5 oz) tuna in oil, drained

1. In a large saucepan of boiling water, cook the green beans 2 minutes, until just tender. Drain and transfer to a bowl of ice water to stop cooking and cool. When beans have cooled, pat dry and set aside.
2. Pierce the bottom of each egg. Fill water in the measuring container to the "Hard" line and pour into the cooker. Place the eggs in the boiling tray bottom-side up. Cover and press the Power button. When the cooker beeps, transfer eggs to a bowl of cold water until cool enough to handle. Peel eggs under cold running water; dry with a paper towel. Cut into wedges. Set aside.
3. Meanwhile, in a medium bowl, whisk together the vinegar, shallots, mustard, salt and pepper, then slowly whisk in the oil until emulsified. Whisk in the parsley.
4. Arrange the lettuce leaves on 4 serving plates. Add 1/2 cup quinoa to the center of each leaf. Arrange the cherry tomatoes, sun-dried tomatoes, olives and tuna around the quinoa. Drizzle vinaigrette over everything. Serve immediately.

Mixed Greens, Rosemary Beets and Dijon Mint Dressing

In this delectable salad, baby beets are steamed in the egg cooker with rosemary and then tossed with maple syrup. They then grace a salad of baby spinach and kale, tomatoes, cucumbers and a medium-boiled egg followed by a Dijon mint dressing.

Makes 1 to 2 Servings

2	baby beets, washed with 2 inches stem and tail end on
1 tbsp	virgin olive oil
1 tbsp	rosemary leaves
2 tsp	pure maple syrup
1	egg
2 tbsp	white wine vinegar
1 tbsp	Dijon mustard
1 tbsp	chopped fresh mint
	Freshly ground black pepper
2 cups	baby spinach and kale
1	roma tomato, coarsely chopped
1/2	cucumber, peeled and coarsely chopped

1. Rub beets with olive oil. Sprinkle with the rosemary. Using a fork, poke the beets all over. Transfer beets to the omelet (poaching) bowl. Fill water in the measuring container to the "Omelet/Poached" line and pour into the cooker. Transfer omelet bowl onto the boiling tray. Cover and press the Power button. When the cooker beeps, remove beets and let stand until cool enough to handle. Peel beets and remove stem ends. Chop beets and drizzle with maple syrup. Set aside.
2. Pierce the bottom of the egg. Fill water in the measuring container to the "Medium" line and pour into the cooker. Place the egg in the boiling tray bottom-side up. Cover and press the Power button. When the cooker beeps, transfer eggs to a bowl of cold water until cool enough to handle. Peel eggs under cold running water; dry with a paper towel. Coarsely chop eggs.

(Continued on next page)

Mixed Greens, Rosemary Beets and Dijon Mint Dressing (continued)

3. Meanwhile, in a small bowl, combine vinegar, mustard and mint, mixing well. Season with pepper.
4. Arrange spinach and kale in a salad bowl. Top with beets, egg, tomato and cucumber. Drizzle with dressing. Serve immediately.

Tip
* Use kitchen gloves when handling beets to avoid staining your hands.

Refreshing Egg Salad

While there are most likely thousands of egg salad recipes out there, when you find one you truly love, it becomes your go-to recipe and all the other ones disappear. Well this one is deserving of your attention.

Makes 4 Servings

6	eggs
1/4 cup	real mayonnaise
1-1/2 tsp	lemon juice
1	rib celery, finely chopped
2	green onions, white and light green sections thinly sliced
	Kosher salt and freshly ground black pepper

1. Pierce the bottom of each egg. Fill water in the measuring container to the "Hard" line and pour into the cooker. Place the eggs in the boiling tray bottom-side up. Cover and press the Power button. When the cooker beeps, transfer eggs to a bowl of cold water until cool enough to handle. Peel eggs under cold running water; dry with a paper towel. Coarsely chop eggs
2. In a medium bowl, combine eggs, mayonnaise, lemon juice, celery and green onions, mashing together with a potato masher or firm whisk, until your desired consistency. Season with salt and pepper, mixing well. Egg salad can be served immediately or stored in an airtight container in the refrigerator for up to 3 days.

Tip
* Serve egg salad in a sandwich or inside a roasted Portobello mushroom.

Variations
* Add 1 tbsp Dijon mustard to the mixture.
* Add 2 radishes, grated to the mixture. You can grate the radishes using a box grater and grate over the larger holes.
* *Egg Salad Wraps:* Add 8 romaine lettuce leaves and 1 cup pea or bean sprouts. Divide the egg salad among the lettuce leaves, top with sprouts and roll up. Secure roll with a toothpick, if necessary. Serve immediately.
* *Curried Egg Salad:* Add 3/4 tsp curry powder and 1 tbsp chopped fresh chives, mixing well.
* *Avocado Egg Salad:* Reduce mayonnaise to 2 tsp and add 1 mashed avocado.

Poached Eggs with Artichokes Provençal

This ambrosial dish includes artichokes, onions, garlic and carrots that are braised in a wonderfully seasoned broth and then topped with creamy poached eggs.

Makes 2 Serving

2	large artichokes
1/4 cup	virgin olive oil, divided
1	large onion, cut in half and thinly sliced
1	sliced Applewood smoked bacon, cut in large sections
1 cup	thinly sliced carrots
1 cup	white wine
2 cups	chicken broth
1 tsp	fresh thyme leaves
1	bay leaf
	Freshly ground black pepper
2	eggs
2 tsp	chopped fresh parsley

1. Trim leaves and stems from artichokes. Cut into quarters. Remove choke (fuzz) from center. Set aside.
2. In a medium sauté pan, heat 2 tbsp oil over medium heat until shimmering. Add onions and cook, stirring occasionally, 7 to 9 minutes or until translucent. Add the artichokes and bacon and cook, stirring occasionally until bacon is browned but not crispy. Add carrots and cook, stirring, 2 minutes.
3. Add wine and cook, stirring and scraping bits from the bottom of the pan, for 7 minutes or until liquid is reduced by half. Add broth, thyme and bay leaf. Season with pepper. Heat to simmering and cook 11 to 15 minutes, stirring occasionally, or until artichokes are tender. Remove bay leaf and discard. Spoon mixture into individual serving bowls.
4. Meanwhile, spray poaching tray with non-stick cooking spray. Add eggs to the poaching tray. Fill water in the measuring container to the "Omelet/Poached" line and pour into the cooker. Transfer poaching tray onto the boiling tray. Cover and press the Power button.
5. When the cooker beeps, transfer eggs to the top of the artichoke mixture. Garnish with parsley and drizzle with remaining olive oil. Serve immediately.

Egg Salad Banh Mi

We've made this riff on the traditional by using hard-boiled chopped eggs in place of any meats. The tangy marinated vegetables meld very nicely with the eggs.

Makes 4 Servings

5 tsp	fish sauce
5 tsp	rice wine vinegar
4 tsp	lime juice
1 tsp	sugar
1/2 tsp	crushed red pepper flakes
1 tsp	minced ginger
1	seedless cucumber, julienned
1	carrot, peeled and julienned
1/4 cup	packed fresh cilantro, leaves torn off and stems minced
1/2 cup	real mayonnaise
1/2 tsp	Sriracha sauce
6	eggs
4	small baguettes, cut in half horizontally
1	small jalapeño, seeded and very thinly sliced (optional)

1. In a small bowl, combine the fish sauce, vinegar, lime juice, sugar, pepper flakes, ginger and garlic, mixing well. In a medium non-reactive bowl, add the cucumbers, carrots and cilantro stems. Pour sauce over vegetables and toss to combine. Set aside to marinate.
2. In another small bowl, combine the mayonnaise and Sriracha, mixing well. Cover and set aside.
3. Preheat oven to 400° F. Toast baguettes for 5 minutes or until browned.
4. Meanwhile, pierce the bottom of each egg. Fill water in the measuring container to the "Hard" line and pour into the cooker. Place the eggs in the boiling tray bottom-side up. Cover and press the Power button. When the cooker beeps, transfer eggs to a bowl of cold water until cool enough to handle. Peel eggs under cold running water; dry with a paper towel. Coarsely chop eggs.
5. Spread mayonnaise mixture on cut sides of baguettes. Drain vegetables. Arrange equal amounts of eggs and slaw among baguettes. Garnish with cilantro leaves and jalapeños (if using). Cover with tops of baguettes. Serve immediately.

Cobb Salad With Garlic Dijon Vinaigrette

This is one of my favorite all time salads because of the bounty of great toppings from crunchy to creamy to crisp. I've topped this one with a Dijon vinaigrette but of course you can always add the more traditional bleu cheese dressing if you prefer.

Makes 4 Servings

2 tbsp	red wine vinegar
1 tbsp	lemon juice
1 tsp	Dijon mustard
1 tsp	Worcestershire sauce
1	clove garlic, minced
1/4 tsp	kosher salt
1/4 tsp	freshly ground black pepper
3 tbsp	extra virgin olive oil
3	eggs
6 cups	coarsely chopped romaine lettuce
2 cups	watercress, thick stems removed
2 cups	seeded and diced tomatoes (about 2 medium)
1/2	avocado, diced
8	slices bacon, cooked and crumbled
1 cup	cooked diced chicken breast
1/2 cup	crumbled bleu cheese or roquefort

1. In a small bowl, combine vinegar, lemon juice, Dijon, Worcestershire, garlic, salt and pepper, whisking well. Slowly whisk in oil until emulsified. Set aside.
2. Pierce the bottom of each egg. Fill water in the measuring container to the "Hard" line and pour into the cooker. Place the eggs in the boiling tray bottom-side up. Cover and press the Power button. When the cooker beeps, transfer eggs to a bowl of cold water until cool enough to handle. Peel eggs under cold running water; dry with a paper towel. Chop eggs.

(Continued on next page)

Cobb Salad With Garlic Dijon Vinaigrette (continued)

3. In a large bowl, combine the romaine, watercress and 2/3 of the vinaigrette, tossing well. Divide the dressed greens among 4 large serving plates. Divide and arrange tomatoes on top in a row down the middle. In rows on either side of the tomatoes, arrange the avocado, eggs, bacon, chicken and cheese. Drizzle with the remaining dressing and serve.

Variations
* Substitute 1/4 lb cooked ham, cut into 1/4 inch strip in place of the bacon.
* Substitute 1/2 lb cooked and peeled medium-large (36/40 count) shrimp for the chicken.
* Substitute Bleu Cheese Dressing for the Garlic Dijon Vinaigrette.

Chunky Deli Potato Salad

Everyone loves a great potato salad for backyard barbeques, picnics, potlucks or just a cool summertime salad. This deli-style salad has just the right balance of potatoes, crunchy veggies and a tangy dressing to be a winner.

Makes 8 Servings

1 lb	gold potatoes, halved
6	eggs
8	baby dill pickles, coarsely chopped
1	small onion, chopped
2	celery ribs, chopped
6	small radishes, thinly sliced
1 cup	salad dressing, such as Miracle Whip, or real mayonnaise
1 tbsp	milk
1 tsp	prepared yellow mustard
1/2 tsp	dill pickle juice
1/2 tsp	granulated sugar
1/4 tsp	kosher salt
1/4 tsp	freshly ground black pepper
	Paprika

1. In a medium stock pot, add potatoes and cover with water. Bring to a boil over medium-high heat. Reduce heat to medium, cover and simmer 10 to 12 minutes or until fork-tender. Drain. Set aside to cool.
2. Meanwhile, pierce the bottom of each egg. Fill water in the measuring container to the "Hard" line and pour into the cooker. Place the eggs in the boiling tray bottom-side up. Cover and press the Power button. When the cooker beeps, transfer eggs to a bowl of cold water until cool enough to handle. Peel eggs under cold running water; dry with a paper towel. Coarsely chop 4 eggs and cut 2 eggs into wedges.
3. In a large bowl, combine the potatoes, chopped eggs, pickles, onion, celery and radishes.
4. In a small bowl, combine the salad dressing, milk, mustard, pickle juice, sugar, salt and pepper, mixing well. Pour mixture over potatoes, stirring well. Transfer mixture to a serving bowl. Arrange eggs wedges over the top. Garnish with paprika. Cover and refrigerate 3 to 4 hours before serving.

Hearty Ham, Cheddar and Asparagus Bake

A warm creamy combination of cheddar cheese, ham, eggs and asparagus gets a whisper of cayenne pepper which is then served over warm buttermilk biscuits.

Makes 6 Servings

3/4 lb	fresh asparagus, trimmed and cut into 1/2 inch pieces
1/2 cup	butter, cut into chunks
1/2 cup	all-purpose flour
2-2/3 cups	milk
1-1/4 cups	chicken broth
3/4 lb	cubed cooked ham
3/4 cup	shredded cheddar cheese
6	eggs
1/8 tsp	cayenne pepper
8	buttermilk biscuits, cut in half horizontally and warmed (see Tip)

1. In a medium saucepan, add 3 cups of water and bring to a boil over medium-high heat. Add asparagus, reduce heat to medium and cook 5 to 6 minutes or until tender. Drain and set aside. Rinse and wipe pan dry.
2. Meanwhile, pierce the bottom of each egg. Fill water in the measuring container to the "Hard" line and pour into the cooker. Place the eggs in the boiling tray bottom-side up. Cover and press the Power button. When the cooker beeps, transfer eggs to a bowl of cold water until cool enough to handle. Peel eggs under cold running water; dry with a paper towel. Cut into quarters.
3. In the medium saucepan, add the butter and cook over medium heat until just bubbling. Add the flour, stirring, 1 minute or until smooth. Add milk and broth, stirring, increase heat to medium-high and bring to a boil. Cook, stirring, for 2 minutes. Add ham and cheese and cook, stirring, until cheese is melted. Add asparagus, eggs and cayenne and cook, stirring, until heated through. Arrange biscuits on serving plates. Spoon ham and cheese mixture over biscuits. Serve immediately.

Tip
* Use refrigerated buttermilk biscuits and prepare according to package directions. You can also make biscuits from scratch or purchase pre-made from your bakery.

Zesty Hash Brown, Bacon and Egg Strata

Enjoy this comfort food dish layered with hash browns, bacon, eggs and cheese for dinner on a cool fall night or enjoy if for brunch too.

Makes 6 Servings

8-inch square glass baking dish, sprayed with non-stick cooking spray

1/2 lb	thick-sliced bacon, cut into 2 inch pieces
1 lb	frozen shredded hash brown potatoes
1/4 cup	chopped green onions, white and light green parts only, divided
6	eggs
1-1/2 cup	shredded sharp cheddar cheese
8 tsp	butter
2 tbsp	all-purpose flour
3/4 cup	sour cream, divided
7/8 cup	milk
1 tsp	Cajun seasoning
1 tbsp	chopped chives

1. Preheat oven to 375°F.
2. In a large skillet over medium heat, cook bacon until crisp. Transfer bacon to a paper towel-lined plate. Discard all but 2 tbsp bacon drippings. Add hash browns and 3 tbsp onions and cook, stirring frequently, 7 minutes or until golden brown.
3. Meanwhile, pierce the bottom of each egg. Fill water in the measuring container to the "Hard" line and pour into the cooker. Place the eggs in the boiling tray bottom-side up. Cover and press the Power button. When the cooker beeps, transfer eggs to a bowl of cold water until cool enough to handle. Peel eggs under cold running water; dry with a paper towel. Slice eggs.
4. Arrange the hash browns, bacon, eggs and 3/4 cup shredded cheese in layers in the prepared baking dish.
5. In a small saucepan add the butter and cook over medium heat until just bubbling. Add the flour, stirring, 1 minute or until smooth. Add sour cream, milk and Cajun seasoning and cook, stirring, 2 to 3 minutes or until smooth and thickened. Pour over egg layers and sprinkle with remaining cheese and onions.
6. Bake 30 to 35 minutes or until browned and bubbling around edges. Remove from oven and let stand 5 minutes. Cut into servings and transfer to serving plates. Garnish with remaining sour cream and chives. Serve immediately.

Egg Filled Ham and Cheese Corn Muffins

Bake these delectable muffins and watch everyone's surprise when they find the hidden treasure inside. They are a great tasting snack when you need a pick-me-up.

Makes 6 Servings

6 jumbo muffin tin with liners, sprayed with non-stick cooking spray

2 tbsp	butter, softened
1/2	small onion, finely chopped
2/3 cup	finely chopped ham
2 tsp	fresh thyme leaves
6	eggs
1	box (8.5 oz) corn muffin mix (plus eggs and milk for mix per pkg)
1/4 cup	sour cream
1-1/2 cups	shredded sharp cheddar cheese
1/2 cup	grated Parmesan
	Kosher salt and freshly ground black pepper

1. Adjust one oven rack to the middle position and preheat oven to 350°F.
2. In a medium skillet over medium heat, add butter and cook until starting to foam. Add onions and cook, stirring frequently, 4 minutes or until golden brown. Add the ham and cook, stirring, 2 minutes or until browned in spots. Remove from heat. Stir in thyme and let stand in skillet until cool.
3. Meanwhile, pierce the bottom of each egg. Fill water in the measuring container to the "Hard" line and pour into the cooker. Place the eggs in the boiling tray bottom-side up. Cover and press the Power button. When the cooker beeps, transfer eggs to a bowl of cold water until cool enough to handle. Peel eggs under cold running water; dry with a paper towel. Set aside.
4. Prepare muffin mix according to package instructions. Stir in onion mixture, cheddar and parmesan until just combined; batter should still be lumpy.

(Continued on next page)

Egg Filled Ham and Cheese Corn Muffins (continued)

5. Divide one half of the batter evenly among the prepared muffin cups. Place 1 egg, bottom side down, inside each muffin. Spoon remaining batter over the top of each egg, spreading batter to make sure egg is completely covered. Season with salt and pepper. Bake 35 to 45 minutes or until muffin tops are golden. Remove from oven and let stand 10 minutes. Remove muffins from liners. Cut in half before serving. Serve immediately or cool to room temperature.

Vegetarian

Avocado Egg Breakfast Sandwich

English Muffin Egg Pizzas

Simply Sensational Vegetarian Frittata

Scrambled Egg Torta

Herb and Chive Goat Cheese Torta

Spicy Egg Salad Burritos

Chickpeas and Swiss Chard with Poached Eggs

Cheese, Pepper and Walnut Egg Casserole

Provençal Vegetable Gratin

Cauliflower Egg Salad

Vegetarian Salad Niçoise

Avocado Egg Breakfast Sandwich

With this easy and nutritious breakfast sandwich you will be ready to start your day. You won't even want to stop for a prepared sandwich when you can quickly make your own at home with fresh, unprocessed ingredients.

Makes 1 Serving

	Non-stick cooking spray
1	egg
1	whole grain or gluten-free bun, sliced horizontally
1/2	avocado, sliced
1/4	small red onion, thinly sliced
1/4 tsp	kosher salt
1/4 cup	packed chopped fresh parsley
	Freshly ground black pepper

1. Spray poaching tray with non-stick cooking spray. Add egg to the poaching tray. Fill water in the measuring container to the "Omelet/Poached" line and pour into the cooker. Transfer poaching tray onto the boiling tray. Cover and press the Power button.
2. Meanwhile, arrange avocado slices on the bottom half of the bun. Top with red onion rings and parsley.
3. When the cooker beeps, transfer egg to the top of the parsley. Season to taste with pepper. Cover with top half of bun. Serve immediately.

Tips
* Add a slice of Swiss cheese on top of the avocado slices.
* Add a handful of arugula to the bun before adding the avocado for a more greens and a slightly peppery twist to you sandwich.

English Muffin Egg Pizzas

Take a toasted English muffin, pile it high with tomatoes, mozzarella and sliced hard-boiled eggs, pop it under the broiler and you have a perfect after school snack or a quick and easy lunch.

Makes 4 Servings

Egg Cooker
Baking Sheet Lined with Foil

2	eggs
2	English muffins, sliced in half and toasted
1 tbsp	virgin olive oil
4	tomato slices
2 tbsp	grated mozzarella
	Oregano
	Kosher salt

1. Pierce the bottom of each egg. Fill water in the measuring container to the "Hard" line and pour into the cooker. Place the eggs in the boiling tray bottom-side up. Cover and press the Power button. When the cooker beeps, transfer eggs to a bowl of cold water until cool enough to handle. Peel eggs under cold running water; dry with a paper towel. Slice eggs crosswise.
2. Meanwhile, preheat broiler with top oven rack 4 inches from heat.
3. Arrange English muffins, cut side up, on baking sheet. Drizzle olive oil over each muffin. Arrange tomato slices, egg slices and grated mozzarella, evenly divided, on top of each muffin. Sprinkle with oregano and salt.
4. Broil 3 to 5 minutes or until cheese is melted. Serve warm.

Variation
* Garnish with torn basil leaves after broiling. Drizzle with balsamic vinegar. Serve warm.

Simply Sensational Vegetarian Frittata

Not only does the simplicity of this dish make it sensational, but the endless variety of vegetarian fillings make it so versatile and a 'go to' dish for any time of the day.

Makes 1 Serving

	Non-stick cooking spray
1/4 cup	sliced cooked asparagus
1 tbsp	thinly sliced green onions
2	eggs
2 tbsp	milk
1/2 tsp	kosher salt
1/8 tsp	freshly ground black pepper
1-1/2 tbsp	shredded parmesan cheese
	Chopped fresh parsley (optional)

1. Spray omelet (poaching) bowl with non-stick cooking spray. Add asparagus and green onions to the prepared bowl.
2. In a medium bowl, lightly whisk together eggs, milk, salt and pepper. Pour eggs into prepared omelet bowl. Fill water in the measuring container to the "Omelet/Poached" line and pour into the cooker. Sprinkle with parmesan cheese. Transfer omelet bowl onto the boiling tray. Cover and press the Power button.
3. When the cooker beeps, transfer eggs to a serving plate. Serve immediately. Garnish with parsley, if using. Serve immediately or for up to 1 hour at room temperature.

Tip

* Frittatas can be made up to 1 day ahead of time, covered and refrigerated.

Variations

* ***Zucchini and Bell Pepper:*** Omit the asparagus, green onions and parmesan. Add 1/4 cup diced red bell pepper, 1/4 cup diced zucchini and 1 tbsp finely chopped fresh basil.
* ***Mushroom, Leek and Fontina:*** Omit the asparagus, green onions and parmesan. Add 1/4 cup chopped mushrooms, 1/4 cup thinly sliced leeks, 1-1/2 tbsp shredded Fontina cheese and 2 tsp chopped fresh thyme.

Scrambled Egg Torta

One of Mexico's best known sandwiches, the torta is a full-flavored, stuffed street-cart sandwich that is a wonderful meal for anytime of the day. This version is filled with eggs, cheese, tomatoes and avocado with hints of lime juice and cilantro.

Makes 1 Serving

	Non-stick cooking spray
2	eggs
1/4 cup	queso fresco
1 tbsp	chopped cilantro
1/2	avocado
1 tsp	lime juice
Pinch	kosher salt
1	torta roll or ciabatta roll
	Freshly ground black pepper
2	thin slices tomato
1	thin slice red onion, rings separated
	Sriracha or other hot sauce (optional)

1. Spray omelet bowl with non-stick cooking spray. In a small bowl, whisk eggs. Pour mixture into the omelet bowl. Fill water in the measuring container to the "Omelet/Poached" line and pour into the cooker. Transfer omelet bowl onto the boiling tray. Cover and press the Power button.
2. In another small bowl, mash the avocado, lime juice and salt together. Slice the roll in half horizontally. Spread the mixture on the cut side of each roll.
3. In another small bowl, crumble the queso fresco and add the cilantro, mixing well.
4. When the cooker beeps, transfer the eggs to the spread side of the bottom of the roll. Season to taste with pepper. Add the tomato and onion slices. Sprinkle with the queso mixture. Add a dash or Sriracha, if using. Cover with the top roll, spread side down. Serve immediately.

Tip
* You can substitute the queso fresco with cotija or a mild feta.

Herb and Chive Goat Cheese Torta

The ambrosial flavors of the herb and chive goat cheese make this medium-boiled egg torta a truly sensational tasting dish.

Makes 2 Servings

4	eggs
1/4 cup	goat cheese, such as chèvre
2 tsp	sour cream
2 tsp	heavy cream
1	clove garlic, minced
1/4 tsp	kosher salt
1/8 tsp	freshly ground black pepper
2 tsp	minced fresh parsley
2 tsp	chopped fresh chives
1/4 tsp	minced fresh thyme leaves
2	torta rolls or sesame seed egg buns
2	roasted red peppers (from a jar), seeded and sliced
1	avocado, sliced
3/4 cup	slightly packed arugula or mixed baby greens

1. Pierce the bottom of each egg. Fill water in the measuring container to the "Medium" line and pour into the cooker. Place the eggs in the boiling tray bottom-side up. Cover and press the Power button. When the cooker beeps, transfer eggs to a bowl of cold water until cool enough to handle. Peel eggs under cold running water; dry with a paper towel. Let cool. Slice eggs.
2. Meanwhile, in a small bowl combine cheese, sour cream, heavy cream, garlic, salt pepper, parsley, chives and thyme, mixing well. Slice the roll in half horizontally. Spread the mixture on the bottom cut side of each roll. Layer each spread side with 1/2 of the eggs, red peppers, avocado and arugula. Cover with the top roll, cut side down. Serve.

Tip
* Prepare the Herb and Chive Goat Cheese spread ahead of time and refrigerate for up to 1 day to meld flavors.

Spicy Egg Salad Burritos

A zesty egg salad combined with tomatillos, eggs and tomatoes make this burrito the quintessential Mexican take-out food you can make at home.

Makes 2 Servings

4	eggs
1/4 cup	real mayonnaise
2 tsp	minced fresh cilantro leaves
1 tbsp	lime juice
1/4 tsp	cayenne pepper
1/8 tsp	kosher salt
Pinch	freshly ground black pepper
2	tortillas (8 inch round)
1	tomato, thinly sliced
1	tomatillo, husks removed, rinsed and thinly sliced

1. Pierce the bottom of each egg. Fill water in the measuring container to the "Hard" line and pour into the cooker. Place the eggs in the boiling tray bottom-side up. Cover and press the Power button. When the cooker beeps, transfer eggs to a bowl of cold water until cool enough to handle. Peel eggs under cold running water; dry with a paper towel. Chop eggs.
2. Meanwhile, in a small bowl combine mayonnaise, cilantro, lime juice, cayenne, salt and pepper, mixing well. Stir in eggs.
3. Arrange tomatoes and tomatillos in the center of each tortilla. Spoon egg salad over the top. Roll up tortilla, folding in sides as you roll. Serve immediately.

Tips
* Tortillas can be tightly wrapped in foil and refrigerated for up to 5 days or frozen for up to 3 months. If frozen, defrost overnight in the refrigerator or in the microwave. Rewarm before serving.

Chickpeas and Swiss Chard with Poached Eggs

This dish is a mouthwatering, nutrition powerhouse with chickpeas, Swiss chard, seasonings and cranberries that are finished with perfectly poached eggs.

Makes 2 Servings

1 tbsp	virgin olive oil
1	onion, chopped
1	clove garlic, minced
1	chipotle pepper in adobo sauce, finely chopped
1/2 tsp	dried oregano
Pinch	ground cumin
Pinch	ground nutmeg
1	bunch Swiss chard, tough ribs and stems removed
1/2	can (16 oz) chickpeas, rinsed and drained
1 cup	vegetable broth
4 tsp	dried unsweetened cranberries
4	eggs
	Kosher salt and freshly ground black pepper
	Greek yogurt
	Fresh marjoram leaves

1. In a large skillet over medium-high heat, heat oil until shimmering. Add onion, garlic, chipotle pepper, oregano, cumin and nutmeg and cook, stirring, 5 to 7 minutes or until onions are translucent. Reduce heat to medium and add chickpeas. Add in broth until mixture is just covered with liquid. Cook until simmering. Tear chard leaves into 1 inch pieces and add in batches, stirring each batch until slightly wilted. Add cranberries and cook, stirring occasionally, 5 to 7 minutes or until leaves are wilted. Gently simmer, stirring occasionally, 7 minutes or until flavors are melded and eggs are poached.
2. Meanwhile, spray poaching tray with non-stick cooking spray. Add eggs to the poaching tray. Fill water in the measuring container to the "Omelet/Poached" line and pour into the cooker. Transfer poaching tray onto the boiling tray. Cover and press the Power button.
3. When the cooker beeps, spoon 1/2 of chickpea mixture into a serving bowl and transfer poached eggs to the top. Keep warm. Repeat with remaining eggs and chickpeas. Season to taste with salt and pepper. Garnish with a dollop of yogurt and marjoram leaves.

Cheese, Pepper and Walnut Egg Casserole

With this recipe, you can add a unique twist to the same old casseroles. Creamy with a little bit of crunch makes it perfect for brunch or when you're craving breakfast-for-dinner.

Makes 4 Servings

11-by 7-inch baking dish, greased

6	eggs
1 cup	diced celery
1/2 cup	real mayonnaise
1/3 cup	chopped walnuts
1 tbsp	chopped green pepper
1 tbsp	chopped onion
1/2 tsp	kosher salt
1/4 tsp	freshly ground black pepper
3/4 cup	shredded cheddar cheese
1/3 cup	crushed potato chips (optional)

1. Pierce the bottom of each egg. Fill water in the measuring container to the "Hard" line and pour into the cooker. Place the eggs in the boiling tray bottom-side up. Cover and press the Power button. When the cooker beeps, transfer eggs to a bowl of cold water until cool enough to handle. Peel eggs under cold running water; dry with a paper towel. Chop eggs.
2. Preheat oven to 375°F.
3. In a large bowl, combine eggs, celery, mayonnaise, walnuts, green pepper, onions, salt and pepper, mixing well. Transfer to prepared baking dish. Sprinkle with cheese and potato chips (if using). Bake for 25 minutes or until heated through. Serve immediately.

> *Make Ahead*
> * *1 Day Ahead of Time:* The casserole can be made 1 day ahead of time. Omit the potato chips. Cover and refrigerate. Remove from refrigerator and let stand 30 minutes before baking. Sprinkle with chips and bake for 35 minutes or until heated through.

Provençal Vegetable Gratin

Layers of vegetables, onions, tomatoes, eggs and cheese make a comforting fall vegetable dish. You can serve this as a main dish or as a side dish. You could serve it as a side dish and then save your leftovers for a mid-week lunch.

Makes 6 Servings

Six 6-oz gratin baking dishes, sprayed with non-stick cooking spray

1/4 cup	peeled garlic cloves
1/2 cup	heavy cream
	Kosher salt and freshly ground black pepper
1	small zucchini, sliced 1/4 inch thick
1	small yellow squash. sliced 1/4 inch thick
1/2	red onion, sliced 1/4 inch thick
3-1/2 tbsp	Virgin olive oil
1/2 cup	bread crumbs
1/2 cup	grated parmesan cheese
1/2 cup	basil leaves, chiffonade (see tip)
6	eggs
1	roma tomato, sliced

1. Add garlic to a small saucepan, cover with water and bring to boil over medium-high heat. Drain. Cover garlic with fresh water and simmer over medium heat 6 to 9 minutes or until garlic is tender. Drain. Transfer garlic to a blender and add cream, blending until pureed. Return mixture to saucepan and over low heat, cook, stirring, 5 minutes or until slightly reduced. Let cool.
2. In a medium bowl, add zucchini, squash, onion and 1-1/2 tbsp olive oil, tossing to combine. Season with salt and pepper. In a large grill pan over medium-high heat, add vegetables and cook, turning occasionally, 5 minutes or until soft.

(Continued on next page)

Provençal Vegetable Gratin (continued)

3. Meanwhile, pierce the bottom of each egg. Fill water in the measuring container to the "Hard" line and pour into the cooker. Place the eggs in the boiling tray bottom-side up. Cover and press the Power button. When the cooker beeps, transfer eggs to a bowl of cold water until cool enough to handle. Peel eggs under cold running water; dry with a paper towel. Slice eggs.
4. Preheat oven to 350°F.
5. In a small bowl, combine bread crumbs and 2 tbsp oil, tossing well. Set aside.
6. To assemble the gratins, evenly divide squash and arrange on the bottom of each gratin. Sprinkle each with 1 tsp cheese and 1 tsp basil. Evenly divide onions and arrange on top of cheese and basil layer. Arrange sliced eggs on the top of the onions. Drizzle each with garlic cream sauce, remaining basil, tomato slices and remaining cheese. Garnish with bread crumbs.
7. Bake for 15 to 20 minutes or until edges are browned and bubbly. Serve immediately.

Tips
* Any type of oven-proof baking dish, with low sides will work if you do not have individual gratin dishes.
* To chiffonade basil, stack basil leaves and roll up tightly. Thinly slice basil across the roll. Unfold basil strips.

Cauliflower Egg Salad

You will love the refreshing taste and crunchy texture or the cauliflower florets, carrot, celery, radishes, pickles and olive in this unique and mouthwatering salad.

Makes 8 Servings

1	medium head cauliflower florets
1	medium carrot, chopped
2	eggs
4	green onions, white and light green parts chopped
1	rib celery, chopped
1/4 cup	pitted green olives, halved lengthwise
1/4 cup	thinly sliced radishes
1/4 cup	chopped dill pickle
1/4 cup	real mayonnaise
1 tbsp	Dijon mustard
1/4 tsp	kosher salt
1/8 tsp	freshly ground black pepper

1. In a large saucepan, fitted with a steamer basket, add water to just below the steamer basket. Add florets to basket, bring water to a boil over medium-high heat and cook, covered 5 to 8 minutes or until cauliflower is crisp tender. Drain. Plunge in to a bowl of cold water. Let stand until cool. Drain and pat dry.
2. Meanwhile, pierce the bottom of each egg. Fill water in the measuring container to the "Hard" line and pour into the cooker. Place the eggs in the boiling tray bottom-side up. Cover and press the Power button. When the cooker beeps, transfer eggs to a bowl of cold water until cool enough to handle. Peel eggs under cold running water; dry with a paper towel. Coarsely chop eggs.
3. In a large bowl, add cauliflower, carrots, eggs, onions, celery, olives, radishes and pickle.
4. In a small bowl, combine mayonnaise, mustard, salt and pepper, mixing well. Add to cauliflower mixture; toss to coat. Refrigerate until ready to serve and up to 1 day.

Vegetarian Salad Niçoise

This salad takes a break from the traditional with protein-packed kidney beans in place of the tuna along with the traditional bounty of tasty vegetables.

Makes 6 Servings

1/4 cup	cider vinegar
2 tsp	minced fresh parsley
2 tsp	minced fresh tarragon
1 tsp	Dijon mustard
1	clove garlic, minced
1/4 tsp	freshly ground black pepper
1/8 tsp	kosher salt
1/3 cup	virgin olive oil
1 lb	small red potatoes, halved
1 lb	fresh asparagus, trimmed
1/2 lb	fresh green beans, trimmed
1	can (16 oz) red kidney beans, rinsed and drained
6	large leaves romaine lettuce, torn
6	eggs
1	jar (6.5 oz) marinated quartered artichoke hearts, drained
1/2 cup	niçoise or kalamata olives

1. In a small bowl, combine vinegar, parsley, tarragon, mustard, garlic, pepper and salt, whisking well. Slow whisk in olive oil until emulsified.
2. In a medium stock pot, add potatoes and cover with water. Bring to a boil over medium-high heat. Reduce heat to medium, cover and simmer 10 to 12 minutes or until fork-tender. Drain. Transfer to a large bowl. Drizzle with 1 tbsp vinaigrette, tossing to coat. Set aside.
3. In the same stock pot, add 4 cups of water and bring to a boil over medium-high heat. Add asparagus, reduce heat to medium and cook 3 to 4 minutes or until crisp-tender. Transfer asparagus to a bowl of cold water. Let stand until cool. Drain and pat dry. Return water to a boil. Add green beans, reduce heat to medium and simmer for 4 to 5 minutes or until crisp-tender. Transfer beans to a bowl of cold water. Let stand until cool. Drain and pat dry.

(Continued on next page)

Vegetarian Salad Niçoise (continued)

4. Meanwhile, pierce the bottom of each egg. Fill water in the measuring container to the "Hard" line and pour into the cooker. Place the eggs in the boiling tray bottom-side up. Cover and press the Power button. When the cooker beeps, transfer eggs to a bowl of cold water until cool enough to handle. Peel eggs under cold running water; dry with a paper towel. Cut eggs into wedges.
5. In a medium bowl, combine kidney beans, onion and 1 tbsp vinaigrette, tossing to coat.
6. Divide lettuce among serving plates. Arrange potatoes, asparagus, green beans, kidney beans, onions, eggs, artichoke hearts and olives over each serving. Drizzle with remaining vinaigrette. Serve immediately.

Variation
* For a non-vegetarian version, substitute 1 can (4.5 oz) tuna in water, drained for the kidney beans.